Field Trips and
Rabbit Trails

through Christianity

Following God's trails without getting lost.

by David Buisch

Table of Contents

Forward

"Blessed be the God and Father of our Lord Jesus Christ, who has blessed us with every spiritual blessing in the heavenly places **in Christ**, just as He (the Father) **chose us in Him (Christ) before the foundation of the world**, that we should be holy and without blame before Him (the Father) in love, having predestined us to adoption as sons by Jesus Christ to Himself (the Father) according to the good pleasure of His will, to the praise of the glory of His grace by which He made us accepted in the Beloved."
(Ephesians 1:4-6 emphasis added)

> "Nevertheless, the solid foundation of God stands, having this seal: **'The Lord knows those who are his...'**" (2 Timothy 2:19 emphasis added).

I have lived a lifetime in the reality of the words above; God's all-knowing and determined will, although spending a third of that time failing to understand the significance of it. I was in my thirties when I first realized my substance was known by my heavenly Father before it was formed. How amazing is that! How many times did I read those words before the truth penetrated my heart?

You will walk in to and out of my life through certain segments of it, used as a segue to Biblical truth. Having walked through the valley of the shadow of death a few times, I know that I am kept by the power of God: So, I am still here by His grace for such a time as this, as are you if you are reading this book.

It is that sense of purpose, and inspiration of the Holy Spirit that has enabled me to put pen to paper, so to speak, conveying the truths contained in the pages that follow. You will find they are centered in and on the person of Christ Jesus and the plan and purpose God established before the foundation of the world in which we live. May our Father's purpose in its publication be accomplished - to Him be glory for ever and ever!

Introduction

We live in a complex environment today, created by man[1] reflecting his anxiety, uncertainty of the future, frustration, and in many cases hopelessness. The good news is we don't have to live in a world of anxiety and hopelessness; by that I mean, there is an alternative. I'm not suggesting a make-believe world or fairytale land — I'm referring to "Christianity".

Looking back over the eighty-plus years I have lived both outside and inside the "faith" we call Christianity, and all that I have heard, read and observed, it is amazing to me that we have managed to brew such a kettle of confusion from something simple but none-the-less profound.

Despite the confusion and seeming divisions within the faith, there emerges a central figure and an incorruptible truth that remains unchanged — Jesus Christ — the Son of God, who took on the form and appearance of man to atone for the sin of mankind through His death and provide eternal life to those who

---

[1] Living in a "gender neutral" Society, the use of the words, man, men, mankind, he and his, are gender neutral.

believe in Him through His resurrection from the dead. This is our starting point for these excursions - Jesus, the Christ.

I'm no theologian, no degrees, just an average man with average intelligence. Over the years I have observed that most of us have a natural tendency to create or elevate something or someone to worship. Out of that need we can and do create idols of anything from money to nature and celebrities, sports and entertainment figures - even "Christian" celebrities, to name a few. The Christian perspective based on the Scriptures[2] is that God, intending He would fill that place, created us with that need, which might explain why religion and spiritual traditions satisfy that need for so many.

Depending on the reference source, the two dominant world religious groups out of five basic religious groups including folk religions, are Christianity and Islam. Out of these, hundreds of variations of religious and spiritual traditions have evolved in the world. From these man exercises his free will to choose what he wishes to follow. It is said that 83% of the world's population are adherents to one of them. I am a Christian, writing from a Scriptural perspective of Christianity, with the desire that not only Christians but anyone searching for answers in a world gone mad, might find this helpful.

---

[2] The Scriptures are the complete text of the Old and New Testament writing, also referred to as the Bible: Bible references are taken from the NKJ version unless otherwise noted.

Chapter One

The Field Trip

Have you ever taken a field trip — nothing really planned just leisurely venturing out to explore the wonder of your surroundings? Well years ago, my employer (a German Company) sent me to Göttingen, Germany, to study the German language. Göttingen was a university Town then (today a City) located about 60 miles south of Hanover, chartered in the 1200's and noted for its historic 14th century buildings; it looked like a page out of history.

The group of students in the class came from various European and Scandinavian countries. Conversation was difficult since I only spoke English. However, I somehow found myself hanging out with four students from Sweden during our free time. I soon learned the attraction to the "American" was a greater interest in practicing their English than German, but they were good company and fun to be with, though my German suffered.

It was Saturday, a beautiful sunny day and the Swedes were otherwise occupied - so I decided it was a perfect time to take a field trip into the inviting countryside. The outskirts of the Town had several pathways maintained for walking, each bearing a name with strategically placed arrows pointing one back to the Town. Who could get lost!

One of the enjoyments of a field trip is, your senses are aroused - you notice things you otherwise would not have seen. With nothing on my mind but conjugating German verbs, I found it easy to let the landscape pull my attention away from the verbs to the butterflies dancing around clusters of wildflowers and the sound of birds. The sunlight flickered through a canopy of leaves as a gentle breeze kissed the top of the trees — and then, a sudden break, a window to the open sky and white wispy clouds; and a blue like only God can create.

Paying little attention to where I was going, I realized I had come to the end of the pathway and was following a foot-worn path that appeared to divide a few feet ahead of me. In front of me lay a beautiful open meadow, close cropped no doubt by sheep; I could see them off in the distance. Looking in another direction, cows grazed and rested on a hillside. What the sheep left were beautiful wildflowers carpeting some areas.

It was a lazy day and I have no idea what my thoughts were as I walked but they were abruptly interrupted by the sight of a barbwire fence and a weatherworn sign that read "ACHTUNG!" "VERBOTEN" in bold letters, with words in the center obviously warning to go no further. Several yards beyond the fence to my left stood a towering guard post — foreboding and grey, the color of death — it loomed up as a ghostly, somber reminder of another time. I felt chills thinking for a moment of what it represented: A remnant of a former evil that sought to rule the world — an ideology that purposed to annihilate God's chosen people. Turning around the contrasting beauty and serenity of the meadow arrested my thoughts once again.

As I stood there and surveyed the surroundings, I realized I had no idea where I was and where I had come from — looking back it all looked the same, with nothing that appeared to be a path. The placement of the sun told me it was late afternoon. Having no idea where the Town was, I headed toward a tree line that bordered the meadow and followed it in what I hoped was a southerly direction — talk about a walk of faith. It was a gentle downward slope, the trees hiding any sign of the Town, but I kept walking, watching the sun slowly setting. After some time, I heard the faint sound of music. As I continued in the direction of the music, I began to hear voices and then laughter.

Ah, civilization! a beer house and a public road — a welcomed sight!

The field trips we will be taking have been planned to draw our attention to the truth of God's Word as it relates to true Christianity, the world around us and a reality check: An honest look at the organized church.

Before we head out, let's get our bearings — the lay of the land and some markings to help find our way back.

Chapter Two

Christianity

There are a few things concerning Christianity to keep in mind as we begin.

One, that Christ, the Son of the living God, is the focus and foundation of Christianity.

He is the centerpiece of everything God the Father is doing, from Creation to the final conflict between Christ and Satan following Christ's Millennial reign (Revelation Chapter 20); two, that Israel and Jerusalem are the only pieces of real estate upon which God has placed His name and seal. This truth is confirmed again and again in the writings of the Old Testament prophets and the book of Revelation in the New Testament; three, that Christianity is the realization of God's final intervention and unconditional covenant of reconciliation through the sacrifice of His Son and His resurrection from the dead. No matter what trail we follow in our field trips, it will always come back to God's plan and purpose, and Christ Jesus; and four, only God knows and reads the heart of man. He alone knows if a man is truly born again of His Spirit, remaining steadfast to the end. While the Church of Jesus

Christ is without spot or wrinkle, in Christ, the organized church in this earthly realm is a work in progress.

So, how does one define "Christianity"? Simply stated, it is God's once and forever solution to man's sin problem which started in the Garden of Eden. It fulfills His desire for a people who through the obedience of His Son, Christ Jesus, are His own:

> *"For He made Him who knew no sin to be sin for us, that we might become the righteousness of God in Him"* (1 Corinthians 5:21).

The first man, Adam, is responsible for man's separation from a righteous and holy God. But it is God through Christ Jesus, who makes it right. Through the atoning work of the cross, God has a people made acceptable "in His Son"; a people assured of everlasting life through the resurrection of His Son. Finally, a people in Christ who love Him, reverence and worship Him for who He is.

There is this wonderful invitation Jesus extends to all who have an ear to hear (Matthew 11:28-39). No one is forced to accept it, in fact the Bible says, *"...whosoever will, may come..."* The God of Christianity elicits a voluntary response to the wooing of His Holy Spirit; for the individual it becomes a matter of choice.

The name "Christian" was given by the Greeks or the Romans to the followers of Jesus, probably intended as a reproach. It was first used at Antioch. The names by which the disciples of Jesus were known were "brethren", "the faithful", "elect", "saints" and "believers"; the same names are used today in many churches. But distinguishing them from the multitude without, the name "Christian" came into use and was universally accepted. This name occurs but three times in the New Testament (Acts 11:26, 26:28, 1 Peter 4:16). [3]

Is Christianity a Religion?

Christianity is by no means a stand-alone "religion" or system of beliefs as the world views religion; to the contrary, it is a rich, deeply rooted history reaching back to God's relationship with the first man, Adam "In the beginning". I say this because as believers and followers of our Lord Jesus Christ, we are "in Christ", the Son of God, by virtue of the atoning work of the cross and His resurrection.

Our natural disposition is independent, opposing God. A man may conduct his life within the constraints imposed by society for social order and be a naturally "good" person by society's standards, but he is nonetheless sinful, separated from God because of his sin nature: It is not what we do, but what we are from birth. If you don't believe that, watch an infant react to the word "no" — we find the display of temper amusing and laugh, but in truth what we are seeing is a display of the fallen nature of man. Understanding that we are born in sin is knowledge that only comes from the Holy Spirit who works in the hearts and minds of men.

As a Christian matures, he begins to understand that he has not only been forgiven the sin that separated him

---

[3] Easton Bible Dictionary

from God, is saved from the wrath of God to come on all ungodliness, but has been redeemed, purchased outright, bought by Christ — he is owned by Him and no longer his own. *"Or do you not know that your body is the temple of the Holy Spirit who is in you, whom you have from God,* **and you are not your own? For you were bought at a price;** *therefore, glorify God in your body...."* (1 Corinthians 6:219,20 emphasis added).

Christianity is a way of life - allowing Christ to live His life in and through us. This is an important aspect of Christianity, because it is only "in Christ" that we are fully acceptable to our Father;

> *"Beware lest anyone cheat you through philosophy and empty deceit, according to the tradition of men, according to the basic principles of the world, and not according to Christ. For in Him dwells all the fullness of the Godhead bodily; and* **you are complete in Him,** *who is the head of all principality and power"*
> (Colossians 2:8-10 emphasis added).

In Christ Jesus we meet the standard required to stand in the presence of a holy God. Jesus was the perfect sinless sacrifice who fulfilled the requirements of the Law perfectly, who loved and obeyed His Father perfectly. Seeing us **in Christ,** our Father sees us as all He intended Adam would be and more, because we are in Christ.

Does God need fellowship?

As human beings we need certain things in life to have a sense of fulfillment; whether it be family, material success or achievement, whatever — failing to recognize that what we really need is fellowship with our creator. Not so with God - He is complete with or without us! What we discover through God's revelation of Himself in the Scriptures, is **His desire for fellowship** with man (the difference between "want" and "need"); to be man's eternal "Father", enjoying man's voluntary love and reverence in return. Adam was God's crowning glory in creation — created in the image of God, he was to be the father of a people populating the earth who loved and worshipped Him. The conditions of this relationship with God were spelled out in God's first universal covenant - the **Edenic Covenant** or commandments (Genesis 1, 2).

As we know, Adam failed, exercising his own will in opposition to God's authority, corrupting God's perfect order. Self-rule and independence is the sin that entered the world and separated man from God through Adam's rebellion, and with it came death and a curse impacting all of creation, — the world we live in today. God lays out His second universal covenant - the **Adamic Covenant** containing the curse on man, woman and creation (Genesis 3). But God is never thwarted in accomplishing His purpose or the plan He set in motion before the world was formed. He has only one plan (there is no 2 and 3), and it takes in everything, including things we would consider a setback.

We see things as past, present and future, however God exists outside of time, His all-knowing covers every contingency, there is no past, present and future, everything is "now".

Following Adam's fall, God watched and waited patiently for man to acknowledge Him: After all, man had knowledge of God and knowledge of good and evil -

> *"For since the creation of the world His invisible attributes are clearly seen, being understood by the things that are made, even His eternal power and Godhead, so that they are without excuse."* (Romans 1:18-20)

However, what He observed was man's natural inclination toward evil rather than good, *"Then the Lord saw that the wickedness of man was great in the earth, and that every intent of the thoughts of his heart was only evil continually. And the Lord was sorry that He had made man on the earth, and He was grieved in His heart. So, the Lord said, "I will destroy man whom I have created from the face of the earth...."* (Genesis 6:5-7).

"But Noah found grace in the eyes of the Lord" (Genesis 6:8), and the eight survivors of the flood, began the process of repopulating the earth: All this happening in the first 2000 years of man's existence. Here we see God's third universal covenant with man - the **Noahic Covenant** (Genesis 9).

As a side note, those eight people held the gene pool that has produced the amazing diversity we see in the physical characteristics of the human race.

Sadly, man did not and has not changed — his gods were and are today, anything except the one true God.

Our culture does not understand the concept of a "covenant". Our treatment of the sacred covenant of marriage is a good example.

A covenant is a unifying binding agreement: From a biblical perspective, a promise made by God with man.

God is a covenant maker and keeper, so true to His nature He continues to extend Himself -

The **Abrahamic Covenant** - the first "theocratic" (pertaining to the rule of God) *unconditional* covenant; one which God performs. (Genesis 12:1-3).

What we see is man's weakness, unable to help himself, and his natural tendency to look for something he can see and touch, to worship. When Moses was detained by God on the mountain, the first thing the children of Israel did, thinking Moses was not returning, was to build a golden calf to worship.

The **Mosaic Covenant** - the second theocratic *conditional* covenant (Exodus 19:5-8): conditioned by Israel's response. The children of Israel broke their promise.

The **Palestinian Covenant** - the third theocratic *conditional* covenant (Deuteronomy 20:10-15): conditioned by Israel's response. The children again broke their promise.

The **Davidic Covenant** - the fourth theocratic *unconditional* covenant; one which God performs (2 Samuel 7:4-17).

The **New Covenant** - the fifth theocratic *unconditional* covenant; one which God performs (Jeremiah 31:31-34). It is here we see Christ, the Son of God, enter the world of man as man. Jesus, the Son of Man, the Messiah coming to save His people, the Jews. Christ is beautifully described as a cultivated olive tree, the natural branches being His chosen people. (Romans 11:11-24). It is to Israel that the Law, the commandments, the oracles of God through the prophets and the promises of a Messiah were given; but through their blindness they reject Him.

In keeping with the prophetic Scriptures, the New Covenant in the blood of Christ opens the door of salvation first to the Jew and then the Greek or Gentile as promised to Abraham (Galatians 3:8). The Gentile is described as a branch from a wild olive tree grafted into the cultivated olive tree, Christ — all according to God's purpose and plan established before the foundation of the world (Romans 1:16,17).

The atoning work of the cross of Christ Jesus and the promise of eternal life through His resurrection from the dead, is available to everyone. That means anyone who agrees with God's assessment of man's condition and responds through faith in Christ Jesus, becomes a **child of God**. This is "Christianity" and amazing grace! It is the world "in Christ", in which the believer finds himself "safe in Christ", with the sure promise of eternal life. Empowered by the Holy Spirit, his life is blessed and protected from danger. It is a wonderful place of peace, rest, liberty, security, fellowship, school for learning and spiritual growth.

Chapter Three

Does God Exist?

What a beautiful day! *"Father, thank you for the sunshine and that magnificent sky with those white billowy clouds! A perfect day for our first field trip. We are looking out over*

this beautiful meadow of colorful clusters of wildflowers; bees buzzing, butterflies fluttering - surrounded by the sound of birds. Sharpen our sensitivity to your Spirit as we explore what we do know and can know about You, and how we know it. In Jesus name, Amen.

Here we are, already talking about God before dealing with the question. For the one who is already a believer in Christ, the answer is a simple - yes! But how does one believe in someone he cannot see or touch — let alone define Him? There is not a person born who does not at some point in their lives, deal with the question, "*does God exist*?"

Now I would not presume to suggest that we can effectively explore all the wonders of the God of Christianity in one field trip, but if we are attentive, we may see things we have not seen before.

God's Creative Intelligence

There are theories bandied about regarding the universe, earth's origin and the origin of the species; each refuting (though unproven) the Creation account of the Bible. But God says, a man has only to look about and observe the lavish, extravagant splendor of His created world to know He exists; or consider the infinite expanse of the universe and the order holding the earth in place thereby sustaining life.

If that is not enough to be convinced, consider for a moment the absolute wonder of the human body, the engineering feat that encapsulates in a single cell, a complex and intricate design engineered and programed to sub-divide and form a human being.

Some people acknowledge that there must be a higher intelligence out there somewhere, but Christianity holds to the sure knowledge that it is the only one true God, creator of the universe, heaven and earth, as revealed in the Scriptures.

God's Revelation

Everything spoken and revealed by God to man, to the Prophets of old, or spoken and revealed by Jesus to His disciples and the Church, is contained in the Scriptures, the Bible. It is the Christian's only reliable source of information relating to God apart from the revelation of God Himself through His creation.

God defines and describes Himself — and it is a good thing He does because we cannot begin to fully comprehend all that He is. *"**God is Spirit**, and those who worship Him must worship in spirit and truth."* (John 4:24 emphasis added).

God is not "a spirit"; there are many spirits in the world, fallen angels and emissaries of Satan, evidenced by the evil we see in the world around us; but they are not omnipresent. God is Spirit — unseen, everywhere and in everything. He describes Himself as "omnipresent"(present everywhere);"omniscient" (all knowing); and "omnipotent" (all powerful).

He refers to Himself as the "I AM", establishing an existence without beginning and without end, eternal, outside the confinement of time.

He is in existence, a "Triune" being: One being with three entities — Father, Son and Holy Spirit, each described as a person functioning with all the attributes of the Godhead. Three in One! Perfectly united in every way.

Have you ever tried to describe our triune God to someone? Now this is a rabbit trail to follow -

The Triune God

Years ago, when I was heading the church youth group, we came to the subject of the triune God in our Bible study. In my futile efforts to be able to present and discuss the subject in a way they could grasp, I lifted my heart to the Lord and asked for help. Here is what He showed me — a cherry pie — yes, it was a whole cherry pie, self-contained in the crust that surrounds everything in it: I understood the whole cherry pie represented the entity, "God", the Godhead.

Next, I saw a piece of the pie cut out, providing a different view — I understood the crust, the covering and containment of everything inside represented the Father. The cherries, the filling or substance - represented the Son. All the seasonings combined with the juice of the cherries, permeating and fusing everything together - represented the Holy Spirit. I wonder if those young people still think of a cherry pie when they think about our triune God.

Another illustration that struck me in one of my travels was the brightly painted Ukrainian dolls. If you remove the top, you find another doll inside; if you remove the top of the second doll you find a third doll inside. The analogy could be carried one step further, removing the top of the third doll there is a fourth representing the believer "in Christ": Don't misunderstand, I am not suggesting the diminutive sizes are representative of the triune God — an analogy can only be carried so far.

As mentioned before, each of the persons function with all the attributes of the Godhead. Paul writes, *"Let this mind be in you which was also in Christ Jesus, who, being in the form of God, did not consider it robbery **to be equal with God...**"* (Philippians 2:5,6 emphasis added).

Perfect Plan, Perfect Unity

Part of the wonder of Christianity is the way the Christian's understanding seems to open like a rose bud with time spent with the Holy Spirit in the Word of God [4]. While the three persons, the entities of the triune God are equal, there is another dimension to the triune characteristic that describes God — that of an order that exists in His kingdom.

A sense of that order, the oneness and unity can be seen in the 16th and 17th chapters of John's Gospel. Jesus is speaking about the Holy Spirit, the "Helper" who will come to fill His place when He returns to His Father, *"However, when He, the Spirit of truth, has come, He will guide you into all truth; for He will not speak on His own authority, but whatever He hears He will speak, and He will tell you things to come. **He will glorify Me, for He will take of what is Mine and declare it to you. All things that***

---

[4] Another reference to the Scriptures or the Bible.

the Father has are Mine. Therefore I said He will take of Mine and declare it to you" (John 16:13-15 emphasis added).

What we see is the "oneness" of the three entities working in complete unity with one focus — the purpose and plan of God. We come to understand that all things belong to God the Father. He, in turn, has given all things to His Son to accomplish God's plan both to create and to redeem His created world and mankind, fallen and corrupted through the sin of Adam. That was accomplished on the cross, although the redemption of the created world has yet to be evidenced in time; but it is coming.

According to that plan, during the Church Age, that is the time from Christ's ascension following His resurrection until the restraining influence of the Church is removed from the world, Christ has given all that is given Him by the Father, to the Holy Spirit to administer. After Christ's millennial reign in Jerusalem, at the very end when all the of enemies of God have been conquered, Christ Jesus will return everything to His Father.

The atoning work of the cross of Jesus and His resurrection from the dead, defeated the power of sin and death. Satan, the spirit of this world and death no longer has any power over the believer in Christ Jesus, who is given the assurance of eternal life sealed by the Holy Spirit.

There is great comfort in knowing that the triune God is who He says He is, that He is aware of everything happening in this world of ours, everything ultimately serving His purpose and His plan — oh, here we are back on our path, the "Existence of God".

God's Attributes

Some of the attributes of God are described as, incomparable, invisible, inscrutable, unchangeable, unequaled, unsearchable, infinite, eternal and wise. His ways are perfect. His moral attributes evidenced in His relationship to man throughout the Bible are love, mercy, long-suffering, justice, impartiality, holiness, truth and goodness: However, there is a counter-balance — He hates sin, will avenge wrong-doing and pour out His wrath on all ungodliness: *"The fear of the Lord is the beginning of wisdom"* (Psalm 111:10).

Everything God is, is working on behalf of His children, often in ways unseen. He told His prophet Jeremiah, *"For I know the thoughts that I think toward you, says the Lord, thoughts of peace and not of evil, to give you a future and a hope."*(Jeremiah 29:11). Something wonderful happens to the Christian as he grows in grace and in the knowledge of Christ. A quiet, deep-settled peace and confidence begins to rule his heart and mind — dispelling fear and doubt: Evidence of a growing faith. Speaking of faith, here is another rabbit trail; let's follow it –

What is Faith?

Faith as it relates to Christianity is simply the ability to believe in something or someone you cannot see or touch or prove exists. A Scripture reference to faith says,

"God has dealt to each one a measure of faith" (Romans 12:3). In this reference Paul is writing to Christians in Rome, speaking of God's gift of faith to members of the

body of Christ, "quickened" or given life by the Spirit of God.

Natural Faith

However, there is a broader application of that truth. God has so designed man that every person is born with the ability to set his mind on something he cannot touch or see with the hope that one day he will have it. How often have you heard a child say, "when I grow up I'm going to be a ....", and twenty-five years later they are what they set their mind and heart on to achieve. We have a natural ability to believe something, a natural faith, though there is nothing of substance or evidence to support the belief.

A good example of natural faith is the belief in the unproven theory that this amazing world of ours just happened, that this awesome human body came from a single cell that one day emerged from the sludge and began an evolutionary process that has taken millions of years to evolve. It seems to me that it takes more faith to believe that, than to believe that man is God's creation, made in His image — if only considering all that science has learned about the human body and its intricately engineered design.

Spiritual Faith

The Christian's ability to believe, that faith is a God given gift; faith energized by the Holy Spirit. The Scriptures define faith as *"the substance of things hoped for, the evidence of things not seen"* (Hebrews 11:1). To believe the God of the Bible exists, to see and hear Him in

His created world is a gift of faith. Christianity is rooted in the belief that there is only one true God, the Creator of the Universe, heaven and earth — and that takes faith because He is Spirit, unseen. I did not see Him create, but the pure creative intelligence in all that surrounds me, tells me He did. One might say it's the starting point of Christianity because without belief in God we cannot accept the next step; that He, God *"so loved the world that He gave His only begotten Son, that whoever believes in Him [Jesus], should not perish but have everlasting life"* (John 3:16 emphasis added).

That which the Christian hopes for, though having no substance, is "everlasting life", that is, life with God that has no end. How? It is through the resurrection of Christ Jesus from the dead. The evidence is God's promise that we are reconciled to Him if we will believe in His Son: The sin that separates man from God and all the resulting sin(s), forgiven and forgotten through the atoning work of the cross of Jesus. That is faith energized by the Holy Spirit.

Faith is the reason a Christian has confidence in the keeping power of God; His protection and provision, regardless of the circumstances being faced. This is another aspect of faith: It is not what we see happening around us, but what we know to be true of God, who is completely trustworthy and perfect in all His ways.

A beautiful illustration of this truth is the situation in which Peter found himself when the boat full of disciples saw Jesus walking on the water. Their reaction to the sight was fear, but Jesus said, *"Be of good cheer! It is I, do not be afraid."* Impetuous Peter called to Him saying,

"Lord, if it is You, command me to come to You on the water." Jesus told him to come — so in faith Peter steps out of the boat and begins to walk on the water toward Jesus, defying the natural law. All was well until Peter looked around and saw the wind whipping up waves about him; he became fearful. In that moment, having taken his eyes off Jesus, his faith failed him, and he began to sink, calling on the Lord to saveHim (Matthew 14:25-31).

The moment fear or doubt takes hold of our minds in any situation, we can and should arrest the thought and reject it, drawing on the help of the Holy Spirit. The Christian lives by faith. It's easy to say, "keep your eyes on Jesus", but in reality, the enemy of our souls is continually looking for opportunity to divert our attention, causing us to doubt and take matters into our own hands. That is the battle going on through our flesh or old nature: *"For though we walk in the flesh, we do not war according to the flesh. For the weapons of our warfare are not carnal but mighty in God for pulling down strongholds, casting down arguments and every high thing that exalts itself against the knowledge of God, **bringing every thought into captivity to the obedience of Christ**....*" (2 Corinthians 10:3-5).

Whether they be thoughts that open the door to discouragement or depression, a pity party, anxiety or fear, they are not our thoughts as new creations in Christ, "old things are passed away." It may be an old appetite creeping back into our thoughts creating a moral dilemma: We can refuse to own them taking a stand against the intrusion, by the power of the Holy Spirit in us — exercising faith in our position in Christ.

It is amazing to realize...that is, to know we have all the resources of heaven working with us and for us through the power of the Holy Spirit, the very Spirit of the Godhead. *"I have been crucified with Christ; it is no longer I who live, but Christ lives in me and **the life which I now live in the flesh, I live by the faith of the Son of God**, who loved me and gave Himself for me"* (Galatians 2:20 KJ emphasis added).

Notice the wording, "I live by the faith **of** the son of God": That's the wording of the original King James version of this scripture. The New King James version changed "of" to "in" which surprised me — was it simply applying the standard word form, without considering the significance of the change? It strikes me as significant because there is a difference between living by **faith in Christ** and living by the **faith of Christ**: Significant because the faith of Christ is a perfect faith, and we are "in" Him!

John's Gospel records the prayer of Jesus, the Son of Man, who is about to take upon Himself, in His body, the sin of the world: He is going to submit his physical body to merciless beating and the excruciating pain of crucifixion by being nailed to a cross, and death (John 17). In His prayer He speaks to His Father asking Him, *"glorify Your Son, that Your Son also may glorify You."* He asks His father to give eternal life, which is *"to know the only true God and Jesus Christ whom You have sent",* to as many as the Father has given Him, praying for those that have come to Him while on earth.

But He goes on to say He does not pray for them alone but for all who will believe in Him through their word. His last request is that those who believe in Him might be with "... *Me where I am, that they may behold My glory which You have given Me...*". Scripture says He offered Himself up in the eternal Spirit, with perfect faith in His Father to do all that He asked of Him. That is the faith **of** Christ Jesus!

The emphasis on the Christian being "in Christ", is seen throughout the New Testament letters to the Church, yet so many simply slide over the words without understanding the relevance; failing to appropriate all that is ours **in Christ**! *The question is, are we living in that reality?* True Christianity is not our attempt to live a Christlike life: The fact is we cannot, nor does He ask us to. It is living by faith, allowing Christ to live out His life in and through us.

Faith reminds us that we belong to God the Father in Christ. He is involved in anything and everything that touches our lives. Though we are "complete in Christ" because of His atonement, the Holy Spirit in us is working to conform us to Christ's image in this physical realm. We are being *"...transformed by the renewing of our minds..."* that we *"may prove what is that good and acceptable and perfect will of God"* (Romans 12:2), because we are the body of Christ, His representatives to the world around us.

Regardless of circumstances, upheaval or chaos in the life of a Christian, our Father declares He is with us and will bring us through the crisis or difficulty. The Old Testament Book of Job, detailing his life experience, gives us insight into the spirit realm and an example of this truth: Satan could not touch Job without God's permission, which if you noticed was limited — the same is true of a Christian today.

Tested Faith

There is another aspect of the faith of a Christian, a consistent principle throughout the Scriptures. Faith grows when it is exercised or tested. Or said another way, if faith is not exercised or tested, it does not grow.

James writes, *"My brethren count it all joy when you fall into various trials, knowing that the testing of your faith produces patience."* Why is growth necessary? For the same reason growth in any form is necessary — to reach maturity. James continues, *"But let patience have its perfect work that you may be perfect (mature) and complete, lacking nothing"* (James 1:2-4 emphasis added). So, it is with the faith of Christianity. We can read or hear about great men and women of faith and their experience and be inspired by the accounts, but our faith does not grow on that basis.

That truth was made real to me through a very simple illustration: In fact, you may laugh at the simplicity of it. My mom suffered from poor health through most of the years we (three boys) were growing up, coming close to death on more than one occasion. Consequently, she trained us to take care of ourselves, which included learning to handle all the household chores that come with maintaining a home. Being the youngest, I ended up doing much of the work — my brothers always seemed to have something else they had to do. All three of us grumbled about household assignments. Washing and drying dishes was one thing, a common chore for kids back then, but none of our friends had to do housework.

It was years later my mom told me she wanted us to be capable of taking care of ourselves if she died.

During times my mom would be confined to bed, all the household chores fell on me. She taught me how to iron a shirt — my father was fastidious regarding his clothes so no wrinkles in his work shirts which had to be ironed. I came to appreciate all I learned from her; I was the only one in my Company at Navy boot camp that knew how to iron clothes (had I been smarter, I could have made a fortune).

Naturally, I followed her example in setting up housekeeping for myself. I found myself buying the same products she used — after all, they must be good because she used them. Considering this aspect of faith, it occurred to me that I could talk all day about my mother's faith or confidence in a particular product; but what of my own? It was not until I used the product myself, that I could say I had faith or confidence in it.

If we have wondered why our Father gives us endless opportunity to exercise our faith — our confidence and trust in Him and His word — *"The just shall live by faith."* (Romans 1:17), — now we know! The genuineness of a Christian's faith in God through Christ, is said to be *"...more precious than gold that perishes, though it is tested by fire..."* (1 Peter 1:7). Use of the word "genuine" suggests that there can be a counterfeit — a claim of living by faith, but nothing behind it - never tested.

Steadfast Faith

Today's society is driven by the expectation of "instant" response and gratification: We want what we want, when we want it. That reminds me of the old musicals produced by Hollywood featuring the opera Tenor Lauritz Melchior. In "The Thrill of a Romance" he sings a song "I Want What I Want" [5]; the lyrics are, *"...I want what I want when I want it"*. Those words aptly describe the spirit of the world.

That is not the way it works in Christianity or living in Christ. One of the struggles the Christian faces as the mind is being renewed in the transformation process, is letting go of the things in the natural seen world. We see that illustrated in the lives of the children of Israel who built a golden calf to worship when Moses failed to return — something they could see and touch (Exodus 32). In Christ our heart and mind is set *"on things above"*, we live and trust in the unseen spiritual realm of our Father.

Unfortunately, that does not always stop us from getting antsy when things don't happen as quickly as we would like. We pray and ask God for something, confining Him to our timeframe or schedule. When there seems to be no answer, we are often tempted to help the situation along — that was Sarah's problem (Genesis 16); and the world is still living with the conflict that developed as a result.

One of the signs of growth in a Christian is steadfastness; a faith that holds fast when the answer does not come. It is not that God cannot do whatever He pleases instantaneously, He can — there is nothing He cannot do. However, if we are praying — *"Your will be done..."*, we remain content to wait on His time and His

---

[5] From Victor Herbert's "Mlle Modiste" - Music Henry Blossom, Lyrics Victor Herbert

place for whatever the petition may be: That's the place of rest we have in Christ.

We also learn that "no" or "not now" are answers. Our Father's interest in perfecting our lives while we are here, conforming us to the image of His Son, is based on our representation of Him and His Son to those in our sphere of influence. That work of grace takes precedence, even over our comfort in some cases — testing our trust in and dependence upon Him as we allow Christ to live out His life through us.

Mature Faith

Faith is also exercised in our relationships in the body of Christ. There is a natural tendency that creeps into our attitude toward one another if we do not guard against it; we become fruit inspectors. The Holy Spirit gives us the ability to discern a person's spirit, whether it be good or evil, but eyes of faith see the finished work of Calvary when we look at each other as part of the body of Christ.

We may recognize outward signs indicating someone is lacking spiritual maturity in a certain area of their life, but we are all a work in progress, growing in grace and the knowledge of Christ Jesus. We are called to love one another, pray for one another, encourage and build one another up "...till we all come to the unity of the faith and the knowledge of the Son of God, to a perfect man, to the measure of the stature of the fullness of Christ" (Ephesians 4:13).

I have a saying that was birthed in a conversation with a brother in Christ, relating to our walk of faith in Christ. He made a simple statement that struck me as profound: "We are both sitting here enjoying fellowship, but no one but the Lord knows how far we had to travel to get here." What we see evidenced in the lives of those around us is where they are; not where they could be, should be or will be — and that is what they see when looking at us. We don't know where they have come from, the length of their journey and how they got where they are apart from the grace of God and the work of the Holy Spirit. With eyes of faith, we see where they will be, so we come along side with encouragement, right where they are.

The saying is, *"you can't get there 'til you get there."* We can spend all day wishing we were as spiritual as ... or could pray like ... or as thoughtful and kind as ... or as gifted as ... but it won't get us there. The "there" is not comparing ourselves with others, rather looking to "...*the measure of the stature of the fullness of Christ*" (Ephesians 4:13). The only one who can get us "there" is Christ through the working power of the Holy Spirit in us and the body of Christ, as we submit and continue to look "...*unto Jesus the author and finisher of our faith...*" (Hebrews 12:2).

A mature faith also knows that our Father through Christ, is in everything that touches us. When we hear comments suggesting that Christians should never be sick, or comments that attribute any kind of sickness or suffering to God's punishment for having sinned, reject them. Our Father may allow and use situations in life, even our bodies to chasten or correct us when needed, but the Holy Spirit will make that known to us. The fact is, we live in a corrupt world in corruptible bodies. We are not exempt from the effects of that corruption on mankind - sickness and disease, material loss and natural disaster, which our Father may permit us to go through, always having His purpose and our good in mind. We live by faith!

It is here we may experience and understand at least in part what Paul refers to as *"the fellowship of His (our Lord Jesus Christ's) sufferings"* {Philippians 3:10 emphasis added). He makes another reference to — filling up in his (the apostle Paul's) flesh *"...what is lacking in the afflictions of Christ, for the sake of His body, which is the Church"* (Colossians 1:24).

We would never know the sufficiency of our Father's grace in Christ our Lord, were we not tested in this corruptible body of ours through affliction or persecution.

There is a kind of humiliation in such suffering, like that suffered by Christ, though limited in comparison — *"And the people stood looking on. But even the rulers with them sneered, saying, 'He saved others, let Him save Himself if He is the Christ the chosen of God'"*(Luke 23:35).

This inspired a piece of prose I sent to family and friends (Easter 2020) entitled, "Why Doesn't He Do Something?"

Why Doesn't He Do Something?

By David Buisch
1 April 1999

A stone glistens as the morning sun catches
a reflection in a fresh drop of blood before
scuffling feet erase any visible trace of it.

The Roman soldiers have all they can do to
clear the way of the pressing crowds.
The street is lined with people pushing and
shoving, just to get a glimpse of the spectacle.
Like rushing water, the street fills with
the sea of spectators as soon as
He passes.
Although protected by anonymity,
each face is betrayed by its expression.
Some jeer, some weep, some spit and scoff,
while others simply watch
and wonder -
"Why doesn't He do something?"

What a seemingly endless journey it must
have been,
every step accentuating the pain of the
open wounds on His
back and the thorns pressed into His head —
the loss of blood.
His muscles strain under the weight of the crossbeam
He must carry to the place of His execution —
He stumbles and falls.
Prodded by a soldier's spear
He struggles to His feet and continues the journey.
His leg and arm muscles scream for relief,
as His steps become more and more halting.
No longer bearable, the Master of miracles
collapses beneath His load.
In momentary silence, the crowd looks on

and wonders —
"Why doesn't He do something?"

A Roman soldier pulls a sturdy looking spectator
from the crowd and Simon of Cyrene steps out of
obscurity into history.
For a moment Simon gazes into the face
of the Man
who has fallen, unaware of who He is.
Ordered to carry the crossbeam, he unwillingly
joins the procession making its way
to the hill called Golgotha.
As the procession arrives, the sky is foreboding;
threatening clouds have formed casting an eerie light
on the players of this eternal drama.
The crowd gathers in silence to witness the scene
and wonders -
"Why doesn't He do something?"

The silence is pierced by the sound of the
hammers, as spikes secure His outstretched arms to
the crossbeam.
Slowly the crossbeam and his blood-stained body
is lifted and lowered:
Settling with a hollow thud — a cry is heard
from the crowd.
Another spike is driven through His feet,
placed on a peg in the rough-hewn
stationary beam, and the torturous process of
death begins.

Looking out on the crowd He strips them of their
anonymity, for He knows each one,
loves them and forgives them.
The crowd looks on — some jeer, some weep,
while others watch and wonder -
"Why doesn't He do something?"

He did —

He died for them, for me, and you!

Ah! But that was just the beginning.

In this year 2020, in a world shaken by fear, we will
soon celebrate the Easter season. We celebrate because
death and the grave could not hold Him.
His glorious resurrection assures us of new life in Christ,
Eternal life, purchased by the atoning work of His cross:
Jesus, Son of Man, the Son of God, was that perfect
sacrifice satisfying his Father's righteous requirement
for forgiveness of sin, taking it out of the way,
and reconciliation.

His words echo through the corridors of time
"Come unto Me, and I will give you rest."
Accepting His gift of life, believing in the atoning work
of His cross, in Christ we have freedom from the
power and curse of sin, freedom from fear,
peace in the time of trouble, comfort in the time of
sorrow, joy in the time of distress and His never-ending

love, tender care and protection until we are
gathered to Him in Glory!

We do well to remember the incredible cost
Christ Jesus paid for our salvation.
Though innocent. Pilot finding no fault in Jesus,
still he had him scourged.
Though the Romans normally used ropes to secure
The person being crucified on the cross, they used spikes
When they wanted to make the death more painful.
All this Jesus endured and still cried out,
"Father, forgive them."
What a wonderful Savior!

In these situations that test our endurance, we are seemingly left to the mercy, care and treatment of man, albeit with the knowledge given by God, because our Father has not seen fit to miraculously heal or deliver us. These are the very people to whom we have witnessed to the wondrous unlimited and miraculous power of God to heal, keep and protect us. Why is this happening?

Well, there are situations allowed by our Father, where the answer to our prayer is purposely delayed; as in the account of Lazarus, *"...This sickness is not unto death, but for the glory of God, that the Son of God may be glorified through it"* (John 11:4). These are opportunities to respond to affliction with patient endurance as did Christ — by the power of the Holy Spirit. The reality of our God and Father of the Lord Jesus Christ is *"...all things work together for good to those who love God, to those who are the called according to His purpose"* (Romans 8:28). Do we rejoice as did Paul? Or, do we complain, moan and groan, feeling we have been put upon unfairly? Are we prepared to express the grace we have by virtue of our position in Christ, outwardly, with joy and absolute faith and trust in Him? That is what pleases Him.

Now, we **are** exempt from the power of sin and death - meaning as a new creation in Christ, **we do not sin**, and the death of this physical body cannot negate the eternal life which is ours in Christ. *"We know that whoever is born of God does not sin; but he who has been born of God keeps himself, and the wicked one does not touch him"* (1 John 5:15). This does not mean that we cannot be tempted or will never yield to the temptation of our flesh, which is sin. But as Paul writes in Romans chapter 7, describing the struggle between the spirit and the flesh, *"Now if I do what I will not to do, **it is no longer I who do it**, but sin that dwells in me"* (Romans 7:20 emphasis added).

Paul is not providing a license to sin, rather understanding. The promise of God is that He will keep us; we have only to place our complete trust and confidence in Him, in Christ, by the power of the Holy Spirit in us. We have power through the indwelling Holy Spirit to resist temptation, but if we give in to it, we need to run to our Father and ask for and find forgiveness.

*"Therefore, humble yourselves under the mighty hand of God, that He may exalt you in due time, **casting all your care upon Him, for He cares for you**.*

Be sober, vigilant, because your adversary the devil walks about like a roaring lion seeking whom he may devour.

Resist him, steadfast in the faith, *knowing that the same sufferings are experienced by your brotherhood in the world.*

But may the God of all grace, who called us to His eternal glory by Christ Jesus **after you have suffered a while, perfect, establish, strengthen and settle you**" (1Peter 5:5-10 emphasis added).

That is faith in action and brings us back to the "Existence of God."

The Eternal God

The eternal God of Christianity is so far beyond anything we can fully grasp or comprehend, a truth demonstrated again and again throughout the history of His relationship with mankind and revealed in the Scriptures. He tells the prophet Isaiah,

"For My thoughts are not your thoughts,
Nor are your ways My ways." Says the Lord,
"For as the heavens are higher than the earth,
So are my ways higher than your ways,
And My thoughts than your thoughts"
(Isaiah 55:8,9).

Our God works in mysterious ways, past finding out, His wonders to perform. In coming to know Him through Christ, there is this wonderful sense of being embraced by

His love, grace, and mercy, His forgiveness and a sense of peace and security that rules the heart and mind. Yes, God does exist!

Chapter Four

What's In a Name?

"...behold, you will conceive in your womb and bring forth a Son and shall call His name JESUS (Yeshua)" (Luke 1:31 emphasis added). Jesus asked His disciples saying,

> *"Who do men say that I, the Son of Man, am?"*
> *So, they said, "Some say John the Baptist, some*
> *Elijah, and others Jeremiah or one of the prophets."*
> *He said to them, "But who do you say that I am?"*
> *And Simon Peter answered and said,*
> *"You are the Christ, the Son of living God." Jesus*
> *answered and said to him, "Blessed are you,*
> *Simon Bar-Jonah, for flesh and blood has not*
> *revealed this to you, but My Father who is in*
> *heaven"* (Matthew 16:15-17).

I believe it is safe to say that the most controversial person having lived on this earth is Jesus, *"Yeshua"* in Hebrew. Over two thousand years after his physical death, He remains the focus of public consciousness and controversy. It is suggested there is no book written, including the Bible, that could contain or say all that could be said about Him. Concerning His life as the Son of Man, it is not a question of whether He really lived: Historical writings apart from the Bible confirm the fact that He lived and died. Josephus [6], a Jewish historian was not a follower of Jesus but confirms His life and death. The question when Jesus walked this earth is the same question debated now — who He is? — or, as in the minds of many, who was He? Only in Christianity is His eternal existence understood.

It is unfortunate that much of the confusion concerning Jesus and His life, has been created by the organized church itself. The Scriptures have been overlayed with conjecture and years of tradition, and in many instances literal contradictions of what the Scriptures say, misrepresenting the truth. The result is a storybook concept for many, and a distrust of Christianity for others. We see this in what is presented regarding His birth — our first rabbit trail in this field trip –

The Birth of "Yeshua"

"Therefore the Lord Himself will give you a sign: Behold, the virgin shall conceive and bear a Son, and shall call His name Immanuel" (Isaiah 7:14). That is just one of the prophesies given by God to the Old Testament prophets concerning the birth of Jesus — God incarnate. It was written over seven hundred years before the actual event

---

[6] The Complete Works of Flavius Josephus - Legendary Jewish Historian and His Chronicle of Ancient History.

took place. "Immanuel" [*God with us*], is the name revealed by God to the prophet Isaiah, referring to the Messiah.

Fast forward to about 4 B.C or earlier, the prophesy is fulfilled. A young maiden living in Nazareth, still a virgin though betrothed to a man named Joseph, is approached by the angel Gabriel, telling her,

> "*...behold, you will conceive in your womb and bring forth a Son, and shall call His name JESUS (Yeshua). He will be great and will be called the Son of the Highest; and the Lord God will give Him the throne of His father David. And He will reign over the house of Jacob forever, and of His kingdom there will be no end*" (Luke 1:31-33 emphasis added).

[7]He then proceeds to tell her how it will happen; that the *"Holy Spirit will come upon you, and the power of the Highest will overshadow you; therefore, also, that the holy one who is to be born will be called the Son of God"* (Luke 1:35).

The angel also tells Mary that her relative Elizabeth who was up in years and beyond child-bearing age, is six months pregnant.

The Scriptures give us little information about Mary. There is nothing said about her mother or a father, or her age, only that she is of the lineage of King David through

---

[7] By translation by William Whiston. Copyright 2008 by Master Books.

his son Nathan. Little is said about Joseph. In fact, he disappears from the narrative when Jesus is twelve years old. We are given his lineage which like Mary's, goes back to King David, however through David's son Solomon, the line to the throne. As a side note, the lineage of both Mary and Joseph, though from different sons of David, meet in Zerubbabel, and split again through his offspring. Since we are dealing with writing inspired by the Holy Spirit, we should be content in knowing we have **all the information we need, to know what God is doing**.

We know from the Biblical account that upon hearing the news from the angel Gabriel, Mary accepts what he says and hastily leaves to visit Elizabeth. Why? Was she thinking, "if it is true of Elizabeth, it must be true of me"? What awaited her was the sure confirmation of the Holy Spirit by Elizabeth and within Mary herself.

Mary stayed with Elizabeth through Elizabeth's full term and then returned home. Since there is no indication Mary shared her experience with the angel Gabriel with anyone before — a reasonable assumption is that Joseph learned upon her return (Mary would have been three months pregnant). We learn that she and Joseph have not been intimate in their relationship although it was allowed: Betrothal was regarded as binding as the wedding ceremony according to the customs of that day.

So, Joseph was naturally troubled and sought means to have her secretly put away, not wanting *"to make her a public example"*; a subtle reference to public stoning which was the punishment for adultery under the Law. Here again, God in His perfect plan, quells Joseph's fears through a dream. An angel of the Lord appears to him and says,

> "... Joseph, son of David, do not be afraid to take to you Mary your wife, for that which is conceived in her is of the Holy Spirit. And she will bring forth a Son, and you shall call His name Jesus, for He will save His people from their sin" (Matthew 1:20,21).

Pulling the accounts of Matthew and Luke together, the things confirmed by the writings are Mary's child will be a male; He is to be named "*Yeshua*", Jesus; He will be the Son of God and He will **save His people from their sins**.

The Bible account records the census decreed by Caesar requiring all citizens be registered in their place of birth. Joseph being of the house and lineage of David, takes Mary and returns to Bethlehem, the city of David. It is here Mary gives birth to her first-born Son - "*But you, Bethlehem Ephrathah, though you are little among the Thousands of Judah, yet out of you shall come forth to Me the One to be ruler in Israel, whose goings forth have been from of old, from everlasting*" (Micha 5:2).

Our God, who can be so precise in His Word as to name the month and the day of an occurrence and even the hour, in this instance makes no mention of the birth date of Jesus. Despite knowing that, today children are taught to celebrate the 25th day of December as the "birthday" of Jesus. *"Is that important?"* Yes, because it is not true. The foundation of Christianity is Christ, the Word of God and truth: He is the truth!

The birth of Jesus was without fanfare apart from the announcement and heavenly display given to shepherds out in the field with their sheep. While first being frightened by the array of heavenly hosts that suddenly appeared proclaiming the birth, the shepherds become so excited they make their way to Bethlehem to find Him. There was no star to guide them, rather, going house to house telling what they have seen and heard, they find the baby lying in a "manger."

The manger or feeding trough, was very likely in the home of one of Joseph's kin. It was not uncommon to have an opening in the wall of the house as a feeding trough, allowing care of outside animals from inside the house. The biblical reference to the "inn" too, could refer to the "guest room", the upper chamber of the home Joseph visited; probably occupied by other family members returning to register for the census. We have been so conditioned by artist's rendering of a stable where animals are kept, we limit understanding that would otherwise connect the place of the birth of Jesus with the house in Bethlehem later visited by the wise men following the star.

The Scriptures tell us that having seen Him, the shepherds left glorifying God, telling everyone they encountered what they have seen and heard. The three "wise men" following the star, arrive in Bethlehem much later. Herod's decree calling for all male children two years of age and under to be killed, would suggest Jesus could have been between one or two years old by that time — His age is not revealed.

Compare these biblical truths with the stories we tell our children and the "Nativity" we present to the public. On one hand we pray that people will take the Gospel message seriously yet, in this instance the truth is distorted and covered with a veneer of man's tradition, laying the groundwork for skepticism and a sub-culture in Christianity. Much of the organized church defends promoting "Christmas" with all the trimmings because Christmas draws attention to Jesus, and yes, it does if only for the season. But here's a question — when Jesus told His disciples *"And I, if I am lifted up from the earth, will draw all peoples to Myself"* (John 12:32) — was He referring to the baby in a manger or the crucified Christ?

People like the story about baby Jesus, and regard it as a wonderful introduction to Jesus for children, but what about the Son of Man *"...who was made to be sin, that we might be the righteousness of God in Him."*, and gave His life's blood for us? Have we made the tradition "Christmas", a sacred cow? The organized church should be asking *"Where does the Bible encourage the Church of Jesus Christ to mimic the world?"*

Before we continue our field trip, "What's in a Name?", here are two poems dealing with this paradox - one that interrupted my sleep. It was Christmas Eve back in 1982 - awakened at two o'clock in the morning with the words running through my head, I grabbed a note pad and pencil and wrote the words down as fast as they came:

Christ's Birthday

By David Buisch - 24 December 1982

Did God forget Christ's Birthday?
I hardly think it so!
There's nothing missing from His Word, He
wanted us to know.
There's nothing wrong with Christmas,
the bells ring out the sound
of peace, good will of happy hearts,
as love and joy abound.

God knows this worn and battered world, with
blood and tear-stained soil,
Needs some relief, some respite
from the curse of earthbound toil.

But I object to being told this day respects Christ's birth.
Forgive me if I seem too bold but merriment and mirth of
pagan rites by ill decree do not a Lord's day make.
Oh, celebrate the day - indeed! But not for Jesus' sake.

I'll admit it's easier to mark a certain day -
As long as I remember it, I'm free to go my way
And soon forget the babe new born
whose end would be a cross.
His life a ransom paid for all
through suffering, pain and loss.

How dull and witless that we think
such love would mere impart
A seasonal transition without a change of heart.

There's nothing wrong with Christmas,
a day of love and cheer,
But any day with Jesus, is the best day of the year!

I didn't broadly circulate this poem until 2003. The poem that follows is one inspired for the annual Christmas greeting to family and friends in 2010 — relating to truth and what we are given to know of God's nature and what is acceptable to Him.

Celebrate Christ!

By David Buisch - December 2010

It was Emperor Constantine, who made by his decree the
special day each year, requested by the Holy See. The
holy day, a solemn mass to celebrate Christ's birth,
called the erring faithful from debauchery and mirth.

It was the winter solstice with unbridled merriment that
lured men into conduct from which they should repent.
No matter that Christ's birthday was not revealed to man,
it's said it was concern for souls that justified the plan.

But here's the rub, you cannot join the sacred with
profane, nor build upon a falsehood without losing
what you gain. The well-intended Holy Day with time
became a season; a season of indulgences, and
commerce was the reason.

The tug of war intensifies each year 'tween saint and sinner to see if Christ will be allowed, and who will be the winner. Will partying and pageantry, the gifts and glitzy splendor win the day and public sway with profits for the vendor?

Or per chance the church will see the error of its way, dispel the myth and tell the truth and celebrate each day. For truth be known, it is the Christ the one who came to give His life to conquer sin and death, that you and I might live.

What we need is Jesus, the Christ we celebrate, whose birth was the beginning of something much too great to be contained in seasons quickly spent and set aside: Hallelujah! What a Savior, it was for us He died!

His glorious resurrection secures for us a place, to be with Him forever and look upon His face. I trust you know the Savior, freed from sin and shame, All through simple faith in Him, believing on His name!

Have you ever found yourself wondering why Christ, the Son of God, didn't simply spiritually appear as a man, as often recorded in the Old Testament? The answer is simple, to accomplish His Father's plan and purpose He must physically die, so He had to come in the physical form and appearance of man, with a corruptible body. Scripture says He set everything aside, His glory and exalted position to enter this world as a vulnerable, totally dependent infant: Born of a woman in the form and appearance of man - the Son of Man. That baby born to Mary was a perfect little baby boy. Several years ago, I was inspired to write a poem for my annual greetings to family and friends, with this thought in mind -

Christmas - Just Imagine

By David Buisch - 11 November 199

Just imagine tiny fingers and tiny little toes, a perfect,
healthy baby wrapped in swaddling clothes.
Eyes as big as saucers, were they hazel, brown of blue?
No matter, they're exploring their new world as infants do.

Just imagine little hands that reach for moving shapes and
things or loving arms that cradle Him as mother softly
sings. Imagine dirty hands and knees as He begins to
crawl. Can this be God incarnate, contained in one so
small?

Just imagine little feet and falls, as He begins to walk,
and hear His senseless jabbering as learns to talk.
Imagine tears that fill His eyes from scrapes and cuts and
sores, the kiss and hug of comfort from the mother He
adores.

Just imagine as you watch Him grow, bewildered by His way;
He'd rather read and talk with men, while other children play.
Imagine all your questions, if and when and where and how?
Does He know His destiny, should I tell Him now?

Just imagine that that day will come, you'll look into His eyes
and know that you can't hold Him despite your tears and
sighs. He's twenty-nine, the world awaits God's Word to be
revealed and while you know His destiny, the end is still
concealed.

Just imagine tiny hands that reached to grasp bright shiny
things, now pierced with spikes, and all you hear are sounds
of hammerings. Those little feet that struggled, the first step to
achieve now bear the mark of nail prints because men
wouldn't believe.

Just imagine as you gaze upon His limp and lifeless frame and think back to the stable where you first pronounced His name. You hear the words of Gabriel, echo in your head: **"Unto you is born a Savior"**, is what the angel said.

Just imagine where we'd be today if none of this were true. There would be no **Christmas**, and nothing man could do to save himself from certain death, twice over for you see without the **Christ** of Christmas, we die …. eternally!

Thank God for Jesus, the Christ!!

When the poem was written, the response of many was they never really thought about Jesus growing up like any other little boy. He was every bit a human being with the only difference being — His was a divine spirit and nature having been conceived by the Holy Spirit.

You see, our sin nature is passed down through the man, not the woman. God's command and warning regarding the tree of the knowledge of good and evil was given to Adam. Adam was Eve's head or covering, He was responsible for her. Eve succumbed to temptation but Adam deliberately disobeyed or defied God's authority - he sinned.

God Incarnate

Jesus, God incarnate, had to grow into the knowledge of who He is and why He was here. That's why the Scriptures say, *"And the child grew and became strong in spirit, filled with wisdom, and the grace of God was upon Him.......And Jesus increased in wisdom and stature, and in favor with God and with men"* (Luke 2:40,52).

To the public, He is simply the carpenter's son. But we see evidence of His spirit growing as the Son of Man, when Jesus is twelve years old. According to some historical writings it was customary at that time, that a twelve-year-old boy be taken on the annual sojourn to Jerusalem to observe the Passover. This was to prepare him for his thirteenth year and the rites performed: In Judaism, a thirteen-year-old boy has reached the age of religious responsibility (this becomes a formal tradition of Judaism for sons and daughters in the Second Century - known as *bar or bat mitzvah* today). But at twelve years of age, Jesus already knows the Scriptures, astounding the teachers in the Temple with His wisdom; and I would add, He has also come to understand who His Father is.

One might ask, how can a twelve-year old know the Scriptures? I have read in different accounts of Jewish customs during the time Jesus lived, that a boy began his education in the Tora and the Law at an early age. While not required to memorize, many by the age of twelve could recite portions of both. Think of Jesus being taught, growing into the knowledge of who He is — the Word: *"In the beginning was the Word, and the Word was with God, and the Word was God....... And the Word became flesh and dwelt among us, and we beheld His glory, the glory as of the only begotten of the Father, full of grace and truth"* (John 1:1,14).

You could say that as Jesus grew physically, mentally and in spirit, the Holy Spirit was, figuratively speaking, unpacking all of His belongings and the mature Jesus emerges, filled with the Holy Spirit having grown into the knowledge of all that He is, albeit in a human body. In His youthful zeal He was anxious to be *"about His Father's business"* which He has learned is not that of a carpenter — according to Jewish custom He would have learned His father's trade. But He had to learn obedience, subjecting Himself to His parents' authority for the next eighteen years.

He also had to experience what every young man goes through as His body physically changed from child to adolescent to adulthood; living in this corruptible body with all the urges and demands it makes.

> *"Therefore, in all things He had to be made like His brethren, that He might be a merciful and faithful High Priest in things pertaining to God, to make propitiation for the sins of the people. For in that He Himself has suffered, being tempted, He is able to aid those who are tempted"* (Hebrews 2:17,18).

He went through forty days of temptation and testing by Satan: Scriptures says he was "filled with the Holy Spirit" withstanding Satan as the sinless Son of Man, and now He's ready to begin His open ministry among the people. Sadly, although within the providence of God's all knowing, the majority were looking for someone who would deliver them from the oppression of Rome. They marveled at the things Jesus did, healing the sick and infirmed and raising the dead to life. They acknowledged that He must be from God to do those things and yet, when He told them who He was, many didn't believe Him:

> *"Let not your heart be troubled, you believe in God, believe also in Me"* (John 14:1).

> *"Believe Me that I am in the Father and the Father in Me, or else believe Me for the sake of the works themselves"* (John 14:11).

It was not just those gathering to hear Him. Here He's talking to His disciples, the twelve that have been with Him during the three years of His public ministry. Now before we are too quick to criticize them for their dullness of heart and hearing, we should remember that we have the entire written Word, the Bible at our fingertips - giving us access to the unveiled mysteries concerning the "Christ" and God's plan revealed to the Church. This was not the case for those who walked with Jesus. As mentioned earlier, boys were taught the Tora and the Law, but by the time they reached adulthood, much of that learning was forgotten. The average man depended on the Rabbi's knowledge in the same way many today depend on a priest or pastor. The disciples of Jesus had no written reference only His verbal teaching. With all that we are given to know, what excuse do we have for failing to believe and place our full trust in Him and Him alone?

What Did Jesus look Like?

What of His appearance - *what did Jesus look like?* This is another of the things we are not given to know exactly. There are many images of Jesus, both in sculpture and on canvas scattered throughout the world which form our concept of His looks — although none using more artistic license than the images created today.

What do the Scriptures say? The only physical description is that given by the prophet Isaiah - *"...He has no form or comeliness; and when we see Him, there is no beauty that we should desire Him"* (Isaiah 53:2).

That is all we need to know. From that brief description we can know that He did not look like Jeffrey Hunter, (Hollywood's portrayal in "King of Kings"). The use of the word "comeliness" suggests Jesus was not a handsome man according to the world's standard; as an example, David is clearly described as handsome and ruddy looking. There was nothing particularly attractive or striking in the features or physical appearance of Jesus that would draw attention to Him. The ease with which He disappeared in a crowd would suggest He was of average height and looked like the average Jewish man - he was neither handsome nor ugly or crude looking.

What of His Nature?

So, what was it that drew people to Him? Simply stated, it is who He is and His Spirit. His presence and demeanor as the Son of Man was inviting, in the same way that Christ Jesus is today when we are drawn by the Holy Spirit and encounter Him. His presence exuded all the divine attributes of His nature — love, compassion, grace, peace, patience, gentleness, goodness, — and more. We see evidence of the grace that marked His life in His encounters with men and women recorded in the Bible. It is interesting that the only impatience and anger Jesus expressed was directed at the religious leaders of His day; He reacted strongly to the commerce conducted in His Father's house [the Temple in Jerusalem] and to the priests and scribes, for their pride and hypocrisy.

The Claims of Jesus - His Preeminence

The most outstanding thing that sets Jesus and Christianity apart from any other spiritual leader or belief system is the exclusive claims both make. An example is that the God of Christianity is the **only one true God**: Perhaps a hard saying, but the God of Christianity and the Allah of Islam are not the same.

And what are the claims of Christ Jesus? Well, to a world that wants to believe that there is more than one way to God and more than one way to reach the Father and heaven, Jesus says,

> *"I am the way, the truth and the life. No one comes to the Father except through Me"* (John 14:6).

And in another place, He says,

> *"No one can come to Me unless the Father who sent Me draws him; and I will raise him up at the last day"* (John 6:44).

And in other places the Bible says,

> *"Nor is there salvation in any other,* (referring to Jesus Christ of Nazareth) *for there is no other name given among men by which we **must** be saved..."* (Acts 4:12 emphasis added).

> *"Therefore, God also has highly exalted Him and given Him the name which is above every name, that at the name of Jesus every knee would bow, of those in heaven and of those on earth, and of those under the earth, and that every tongue should confess that Jesus Christ is Lord, to the glory of God the Father"* (Philippians 2:9-11).

The above verses of Scripture make it clear that there is but one source of salvation, Christ Jesus: The Father draws a person to Christ through the Holy Spirit, creating opportunity to hear and respond to the Gospel. That is why there is a risk involved in thinking I'll wait - *"some other time"*, and why His Word says,

> *"...Behold **now** is the accepted time; behold **Now** is the day of salvation"* (2 Corinthians 6:2 emphasis added).

These claims made by Jesus create a dilemma. Considering them, one must conclude that either Jesus is who He says He is, or He is a fake and a liar suffering from delusions. These claims are part of the Christian's firm foundation in Christ and Him alone.

To avoid controversy, the religious world outside of Christianity acknowledges Jesus as having been a good man, a prophet or teacher — but denies His eternal existence and divine nature. Can a fake and liar be considered a "good man"?

The Scriptures describe Him as...

> *The image of the invisible God, the firstborn over all creation. For by Him all things were created that are in heaven and that are on earth, visible and invisible, whether thrones or dominions or principalities or powers. All things were created through Him and for Him. And He is before all things, and in Him all things consist. And He is the head of the body, the church, who is the beginning, the firstborn from the dead, that in all things He may have preeminence"* (Colossians 1:15-18).

Yoked Together

God has given man free will, that is, he is free to choose to believe whatever he wants to believe. He can worship whatever or whomever he chooses to worship.

But there is an invitation that echoes down the corridors of time; one given by Jesus, addressing the crowds of people who followed Him.

> "Come unto Me, all you who labor and are Heavy laden, and I will give you rest. Take My yoke upon you and learn from Me, for I am gentle and lowly in heart and you will find rest for your souls. For My yoke is easy and My burden is light" (Matthew 11:28-30).

That rest is found only in Christ Jesus, in God, based on faith and trust in Him and the finished work of the cross.

I witnessed an illustration of the above Scripture during a visit to the Dominican Republic. Travelling with a colleague, we arrived early afternoon in Santo Domingo, hot and anxious to get to the hotel and the beach. It was a bit of a let-down learning that there was no beach: The coastline was lined with jagged rocks. We learned however, that the Island was narrow and a drive of a little more than an hour took you to the other side of the Island and a beautiful sandy beach. This was where the cruise ships docked. Land tourists were accommodated at a beautiful government hotel that specialized in hotel training, but I'm getting ahead of myself.

We rented a car — as I recall it was small, looked like a bug and barely large enough to hold two people, but we were assured it would get us to the other side of island. The road was fairly decent, lined on both sides by sugar cane fields. As we made our way cross-island, we happened upon a local resident slowly walking along side an ox-drawn cart full of sugar cane. I was driving and pulled off to the side of the road — it was a sight I had to see up close: Two oxen yoked together with a heavy wooden yoke. My eyes were immediately drawn to a magnificent, strong, healthy fully grown ox, obviously well cared for and patiently standing there while we talked with its owner. Next to it, was a younger ox.

My friend was a linguist, fluent in Spanish and in conversation with the man learned the young ox was being trained — learning to adjust to being yoked to another ox and learning to walk being yoked. The young ox was not pulling or bearing weight, not even the weight of the yoke, that all rested on the mature ox. Immediately the above Scripture came to mind: What a beautiful picture of our place, yoked together with Christ.

How many Christians find that place of rest? That quiet confidence that despite the turmoil and commotion in the world around us, we are safe in Christ, in God. It is wonderful to lay the head down at night and sleep knowing there are situations in life only God can change — leaving those matters in His hands with complete confidence! That is faith and life lived in Christ Jesus!

So, what's in a name? Christianity is rooted in the truth that Jesus is "...the Christ, the Son of the Living God! The Lamb of God who takes way the sin of the world.", described by Isaiah's prophetic word:

"For unto us a Child is born, unto us a Son is given; and the government will be upon His shoulder. His name shall be called Wonderful,

Counselor, Mighty God, Everlasting Father, Prince of Peace. Of the increase of His government and peace there shall be no end, upon the throne of David and over His kingdom, to order it and establish it with judgment and justice from that time forward, even forever. The zeal of the Lord of hosts shall perform this" (Isaiah 9:6,7).

Chapter Five

Catch the Wind

Now here is a field trip it seems few takes. *Take a deep breath and enjoy the fresh air and notice the gentle breeze visible in the treetops. While taking in the sights there is a sudden movement of air swirling around you scattering leaves - where did that come from?* That is probably the best description one can give of the Holy Spirit:

> *"The wind blows where it wishes, and you hear the sound of it, but cannot tell where it comes from and where it goes. So is everyone who is born of the Spirit"* (John 3:3-8).

The Spirit of God

He too is a person, the very Spirit of God, therefore the Spirit of the Father and the Son, yet it would seem He functions as a separate entity — or does He? I don't know how many times I have poured over the beautiful prayer of Jesus in the 17th Chapter of John's Gospel. It is a description of perfect unity and single-minded purpose that exists, making it clear that there is never a break or breach in the relationship between the Father and the Son and the **always present Holy Spirit**. It explains why the misuse of the **names of God and of Jesus Christ** can be forgiven, but because God is Spirit, speaking or acting irreverently or profanely against His Holy Spirit, is unforgivable; referred to as blasphemy in Scripture.

An example of blasphemy against the Holy Spirit is found in Matthew's gospel account of two incidents where Jesus delivered men of demon possession (Matthew 9:34 and Matthew 12:24). When the Pharisees hear of it, they say, *"This fellow does not cast out demons except by Beelzebub, the ruler of demons"* (Matthew 12:24).

The Scriptures refer to the Holy Spirit in different ways; the Spirit of God, the Spirit of truth, the Holy Spirit, the eternal Spirit, the Helper and the Comforter as an example, but it is one and the same Holy Spirit. He was present in the beginning *"…hovering over the face of the waters"* (Genesis 1:2). When the Scriptures refer to the Spirit "coming upon" Old Testament men and women, it is the Holy Spirit: Listen to King David praying, *"…And do not take your Holy Spirit from me"* (Psalm 51:11).

Jesus offered Himself up in the death of His physical body through the eternal Spirit, through Whom the Father then raised Him from the dead.

Jesus, the Son of Man, born of the Spirit of God, brought that unity and single-minded purpose down to earth to dwell among men. How? By the Spirit of God in Him, He was *"…born of the Spirit."* His spirit and the Holy Spirit being one.

While Jesus walked this earth in the form and appearance of man, filled with the Holy Spirit, He was "the Comforter" or keeper of those the Father gave Him. As the time of His death neared, He told His disciples that He would not be with them much longer, that He would be returning to His Father. He comforted them by telling them that the Father would send "another" Comforter or Helper, explaining that it was expedient or necessary that He go. (John 16:5-14) We are apt to forget that Jesus, in His human corruptible body could only be in one place at a time, but the Spirit of Christ has no limitation. So, everything belonging to the Father, given to the Son for a time, is given by the Son to the Holy Spirit to be administered by Christ Jesus through Him until the end of the age when Christ establishes His kingdom here on earth.

> *"All things that the Father has, are Mine. Therefore, I have said that He (the Holy Spirit) will take of Mine and declare it to you"* (John 16:15 emphasis added).

The first to receive the Holy Spirit were the disciples of Jesus. They were gathered together after His resurrection, having heard that Christ Jesus was risen from the dead. John's Gospel records His appearance among them in His glorified body:

> *"Then Jesus said to them again, 'Peace to you, as the Father has sent Me, I also send you.' And when He had said this, **He***

breathed on them, and said to them, 'Receive the Holy Spirit'" (John 20:21,22 emphasis added).

The role the Holy Spirit plays in Christianity is everything that serves the Father's plan and purpose, established in Christ before the foundation of the world. If you remember the claims Jesus made, one was *"...no one comes to the Father except through Me..."* and in another place he says, *"...no one can come to Me unless the Father who sent Me draws him...".*

The Holy Spirit is the one who draws us as the Father wills - how does it happen? There is a moment or there may be different moments of sensitivity to the Holy Spirit; intercepts in life much like those in a football game. These are occurrences we most likely attribute to a coincidence - something that cannot be explained; it is a heart and soul tenderness that touches us, leaving us open to respond to the word of God and invitation of Christ. In fact, having come to Christ and looking back on our lives, we often recognize those moments when the Holy Spirit intercepted us and continued to intercept us until we responded. Jesus told the Pharisee, Nicodemus, *"...Most assuredly, I say to you, unless one is Born again, he cannot see the kingdom of God."*

Nicodemus responded from the only reference he had, that of the natural birth. To which Jesus replied,

"Most assuredly, I say to you, unless one is born of water and the Spirit, he cannot enter the kingdom of God. That which is born of the flesh is flesh, and

that which is born of the Spirit is spirit. Do not marvel that I said to you, 'You must be born again'. The wind blows where it wishes, and you hear the sound of it, but cannot tell where it comes from and where it goes. So is everyone who is born of the Spirit" (John 3:3-8).

And so it is, as believers in Christ Jesus and the atoning work of the cross we are "born again", born of the Spirit of God as a new creation "in Christ": Not a makeover, a completely new creation in righteousness. Then, as a resident dweller the Holy Spirit is a baptizer, a helper, teacher and guide, a comforter and enabler. In fact, everything we do "in Christ" as that new creation, is done by the enabling power of the Holy Spirit through Christ.

However, there is a caveat often overlooked — it involves the separation of the old from the new. The Scriptures illustrate this truth in the life of Abraham, when he is told by God to send Ishmael away, his first-born son by Hagar — separating the son of the flesh from Isaac, the son of promise (Genesis 21). The Bible often uses the word "flesh" when talking about the "old nature" which, though we are a new creation, is with us because we continue to live in the same corruptible body with all its appetites and habits and the same mind and thinking. Here is where the Holy Spirit begins His amazing, wonderful work, taking us on a journey that lasts a lifetime here. However, it is a journey that requires our cooperation – let's follow that rabbit trail looking at the life of a "new- born in Christ" as it might unfold from a biblical perspective.

New Shoes

From what I remember and the things I have been told, I was apparently a very sensitive little boy. All you had to do was look at me cross eyed and I cried. In fact, my brothers called me a "blat-baby". My poor mother — picture this, the family in church: My mom sitting on the aisle, me next, then her mother, then my middle brother, oldest brother and my dad, in that order.

It often happened that the pastor would call on my mother to pray. She would stand and begin to pray, and I would stand clinging to her and start to cry. I remember a beautiful dress, light green with a flower pattern and a full skirt — as she prayed, her arm and hand holding me close in an attempt to comfort me, I cried and wound myself up in that lovely full skirted dress, snotty nose, tears and all; all the time my dad with a menacing look motioning me to come to him. By the time my mom finished praying that lovely dress was a mess.

She told me I did not like anything new and unfamiliar, describing the struggle she would go through to get a new pair of shoes on my feet. From what she said I didn't throw tantrums — no kicking and screaming. Apart from curling my toes to make it difficult, my resistance was simply a fountain of woeful tears. I have no idea why I resisted something new but actually remember the feeling of being stuffed into that new snowsuit — the tears were the same, but I could make myself stiff as a board to express my displeasure.

Well, thank the Lord, He somehow delivered me from that, because He had something new in mind for me: A new creation, a new spirit and a clean heart! *"What **might** that experience look like?"*

"Here I am, something wonderful has happened — I find myself overwhelmed by a sense of well-being and peace! What is this feeling? as though a weight had been lifted from me and for the first time in a long time, I feel clean. There are really no words to describe the peace I feel and the love of Christ Jesus flooding my soul."

That generally expresses the sense of well-being we have as a new believer in Christ. Notice the word **"might"** above: Our tendency is to want to put God in a box, that the way He works must be like this or that. The Bible says, *"His ways are past finding out "*, so let God be God. Obviously, we are each one different with different personalities so the afterglow of the encounter with Jesus Christ will be different and His dealings with us will be different. But it is here that the Holy Spirit begins His work in us as we learn to acknowledge and rely upon Him: The key words being **to acknowledge and rely upon** Him.

A newborn baby is vulnerable in the human and most of the animal worlds. God in His wisdom has placed an instinct to protect that new life in the female of most species during the early stages of development. Picture a baby giraffe dropped six feet to the ground at birth. It must quickly, within minutes, get up on all four of those spindly legs because of its vulnerability to animals that prey on the weak. There is little the mother can do to help apart from nudging and once up, steadying it while it learns to stand and walk. It is amazing how quickly it is walking; and before you know it, expressing the wonderful enthusiasm and care-free joy of a "new-born" discovering its new world.

It is no different in the spiritual realm. The Holy Spirit is the protector working through the body of Christ, nudging the new life in Christ to stand: Steadying it while it learns to walk. In Christianity that experience is infectious. To be part of feeding and encouraging a new life in Christ in the Word of God, sharing the enthusiasm and care-free joy of the person growing in grace and the knowledge of Christ during that "sheltered" period, is a privilege and pure joy. However, it is a critical time and vital that they learn that their new life **is "in Christ"**, and to acknowledge and depend upon the Holy Spirit to help, guide and direct them in their walk of faith.

If you have ever watched a nesting bird and the fledglings, you have witnessed when time came to leave the nest. The fledgling boldly sits on the edge of the nest inspired by the view of the expanse of the open sky above with aspirations of soaring to great heights but intimidated by the view of the ground below. Some bravely launch themselves confident they can do what they have seen their parents do while others more reticent have to be coaxed and finally nudged by a parent: *"It is time to test your wings"*. That time comes to a child of God in His plan and purpose for that life.

The Holy Spirit knows when it is time to move on. Like the baby in the natural world, milk is good but our new life in Christ needs solid food if we are to grow and build a solid foundation, established in the Word. If we have been involved, as the body of Christ, encouraging and supporting a new Christian, it is important that we be sensitive to the change, lest we hinder the work of the Holy Spirit.

That reminds me of the baby cardinal I spotted while cutting grass. It was close to the edge of the road making peeping sounds. I saw no signs of its parents, so concerned that it might get hit by passing traffic, I picked it up and set it back in the grass several yards from the road. As I passed the area again, there it was on the edge of the road. It didn't try to fly as I picked it up and again placed it several yards away from the road.

The third time passing the area and finding it next to the road, I decided to call a friend of mine who works rehabilitating wildlife, thinking it might be injured in some way. She told me to examine the underbelly to see if the feathers were smooth: They were, indicating it was not injured. She then asked if there was an area of undergrowth, brush and trees nearby – to which I responded, *"yes, across the road and several yards from the road."* She told me to put the baby cardinal on the other side of the road, that the parents were calling it to the protection of the wooded area. Making the next pass after putting it on the other side of the road, there was no sign of it and no peeping sound; but I did spot a beautiful red cardinal in the brush.

I thought I was helping and protecting the baby bird, but in fact I was hindering it, literally setting it back from the progress it was making. The Holy Spirit knows each one of us intimately and what is needed to strengthen us in the inner man in this process of conforming us to the image of Christ. In the desire to protect newborns we need to be careful to be sensitive to the Holy Spirit, so our interaction is full of Christ's love and compassion but free of the influence of our natural emotions.

Testing Our Wings!

Subtle changes in behavior and attitude have already begun to evidence themselves in the newborn Christian we have been following in this illustration. However, there is an aspect of his life that remained the same, though having come to Christ. It is the world he created before salvation — it is all there, the habits good and bad, the friends, the passions and all the other baggage he carried around.

He might ask, *"How can that be? I thought everything relating to my life before salvation has passed away?"*

> *"Therefore, if anyone is in Christ, He is a*
> *new creation; old things have passed away;*
> *behold, all things have become new"*
> (2 Corinthians 5:17).

Welcome to "Spiritual Warfare 101" - the struggle between the flesh and the spirit. (The Bible uses the word "flesh" as representing our old sin nature, and the word "spirit" as representing our new nature in Christ). We have been reconciled to God; our sin(s) forgiven yet we still live in this corruptible body. Our mind, our attitude and way of thinking must adjust to our new life in Christ and will change as we spend time in the Word and cooperate with the Holy Spirit working in us, to conform us to the image of Christ Jesus.

> *"I beseech you therefore brethren by the mercies of God, that you present your bodies a living sacrifice, holy, acceptable to God, which is your reasonable service.*
>
> *And do not be conformed to this world but be **transformed by the renewing of your mind**, that you may prove what is that good and acceptable and perfect will of God"* (Romans 12:1,2 emphasis added).

"Why does the mind have to be renewed if I am complete in Christ? Being "complete in Christ" is our position before the Father as a new person (creation) with a new spirit and a clean heart. We are acceptable to Him and able to stand in His presence owing to the atoning work of the cross because Christ Jesus meets the Father's righteous requirement. Were we standing on the threshold facing eternity as was the thief on the cross next to Jesus, salvation is a complete work. Our Father sees us "in Christ", we are clothed in the righteousness of Christ –

> *"For He made Him who knew no sin to be sin for us, that we might become the righteousness of God in Him (Christ Jesus)"* (2 Corinthians 5:21 emphasis added).

However, if for a time we are to remain in this earthly realm, we must grow into the knowledge of who we are "in Christ", that the outward expression of our lives confirms the truth that, as John writes,

> *"Whoever has been born of God does not sin, for His seed remains in him; and he cannot sin, because he has been born of God"* (1 John 3:9).

We are not two people as some would suggest. We are one person, born of the Spirit, a new creation living in a corruptible body. What we were, the "old" born in sin, died on the cross when Jesus, who *"...was made to be sin..."* for us, died.

Think of the mind as the command center of this corruptible body. It controls the emotions and impulses of the different members of the body. The conflict between the flesh and the spirit aptly described by Paul in Romans chapter 7, exists because Satan has only one desire and that is to destroy the work of God; that includes us.

Before coming to Christ, we belonged to the world ruled by Satan. Our corruptible body and its appetites, everything about us, our past — conduct, attitudes and passions are known to the enemy of our soul; and he will use any of it he can to temp us, draw us away from Christ and His protection, isolate us, even cause us to question our salvation, deceive us, and if nothing else, distract us to keep us from the Word of God.

There is a certain bird with peculiar habits. Finding a tree with a hole in it, the female enters to lay her eggs.

The male seals her in the nest until the eggs are hatched - leaving only a small hole to feed her during the process. Once the eggs are hatched the nest is opened to release the female and then resealed leaving a hole to feed the young. In one species, there are usually two fledglings but only one survives because it dominates the hole keeping the other from being fed.

What a picture! The enemy of our soul would like to dominate what we feed upon keeping us from the Word of God with the intent that our new life in Christ would die. The spirit is fed by the Word of God. Paul writes, "Study *to show yourself approved...*", reading and meditating on the Scriptures, allowing the Holy Spirit to teach us and open our hearts and minds to truth, giving us spiritual understanding. That is the way the Christian grows in grace and in the knowledge of Christ Jesus. Through the Word the Holy Spirit is working to conform us to the image of Christ, while Satan uses everything in his arsenal to try to keep that from happening.

Watch Out!

There is an underlying truth here that is often over-looked. Satan cannot touch us unless God allows it. If God allows it, it serves His purpose in the same way testing through circumstances come — *"And we know that all things work together for good to those who love God, to those called according to His purpose"* (Romans 8:28). Satan can only succeed in his efforts to undermine the work of the Holy Spirit in us, **when we allow it** because he no longer has any power over us. Whenever he comes at us, most often through the mind, if we will submit to God at that moment and resist him by the power of the Holy Spirit in us, he will fail in his attempt. James writes, *"...submit to God, resist the devil and He will flee from you. Draw near to God and He will draw near to you..."* (James 4:7,8).

While we are in this world, we are part of the body of Christ, representing and presenting Christ to the world around us. Our testimony of the transforming power of God through Christ Jesus, is our life "in Christ" and the way it is lived out by the power of the Holy Spirit. *"I have been crucified with Christ, it is no longer I who live, but Christ lives in me; and the life I now live in the flesh I live by faith of the Son of God, who loved me and gave Himself for me"* (Galatians 2:20).

The question we should ask is — *"is this a living reality in my daily life?"* There are so many distractions in the world — work, family, entertainment and particularly those through technology. The tech toys on the market are designed to occupy a person's mind and attention: Many of them become an appendage, a subconscious dependence, and in some cases an addiction; and that, by design of the enemy of our souls.

A friend of mine was scrolling through her cell phone images to show me a picture. Failing to find it, she pulled up her main page. I was shocked to the point of commenting on the number of Apps loaded on her phone to which she replied, *"I know, I don't know where they came from, I didn't ask for them and I don't use them."*

While there are some genuinely wonderful aspects of our high-tech environment, we tend to forget that the spirit of the world is fostered and controlled by Satan. While knowledge is given by God, Satan uses the knowledge given man to oppose everything that relates to the one true God, and ceaselessly works to destroy His works. The Bible says he comes as an angel of light — presenting something that looks good, seems good and beneficial, but by design leads to bondage and destruction: The things in this world that have the greatest allure, have a hook in them - watch out!

The Spirit of God in us is faithful to warn us of danger if we are attentive to Him. The computer-internet age is full of subtle snares. One is the aspect of privacy — the privacy of home providing coverage for participating in things to which we would otherwise not be exposed.

Pornography becomes a temptation even to Christians: It is easy to rationalize that *"I'm not hurting anyone..."*, when in fact, we become vicarious participants in the sin of others; also failing to realize that what we do does have an impact on the body of Christ.

Another subtle influence is access to knowledge. The internet is a fulfillment of prophecy that in the last days knowledge will increase. Search any word or subject and you will find the information you a searching for. The snare is a common mind-set even among Christians, that if it is on the Internet, it must be correct or true.

Nothing could be further from the truth. Many postings are downright false or half-truths, deceptive, calculated to mislead and designed to side-track us or simply create confusion. There is only one dependable source for truth and that is the Word of God, the Bible. Sadly, there are many in Christianity who rarely open the cover and read for themselves that they might grow in wisdom and discernment.

The body of Christ working under the guidance and direction of the Holy Spirit is in and of itself, the ministry; equipped to encourage, strengthen and correct one another as we all grow in faith, in grace and in the knowledge of Christ Jesus.

Well, we have walked quite a way from our intended path, so let's get back –

John the Baptist referring to Jesus, said, *"...He who is coming after me is mightier than I, whose sandals I am not worthy to carry.* **He will baptize you with the Holy Spirt and fire"** (Matthew 3:11 emphasis added). On the day of Pentecost that literally happened to the disciples of Christ (Acts 2:1-13). The baptism with the Holy Spirit is a sovereign act of Christ empowering the saints to carry out His great commission.

Though the manifestation of the Holy Spirit displayed in that upper room has not, to my knowledge, been repeated in the same manner, we read in the book of the Acts of the Apostles, that Christ continued to baptize believers with the Holy Spirit; in some recorded instances, evidenced or accompanied by languages *(tongues)* being spoken that were not known to those speaking - those being baptized. This initial evidence was significant in overcoming the skepticism of many Jews hearing the Gospel.

The Old Testament prophet Joel prophesied that the time was coming when God would pour out His Spirit on **all flesh** (Joel 2:28,29). Peter, in his eloquent speech to those amazed by the manifestation of the Holy Spirit on the day of Pentecost, remarked that *"...this is what was spoken by the prophet Joel: And it shall come to pass in the last days, says God, That I will pour out My Spirit on all flesh ..."*

So, what are the last days? The "last days" began when Christ Jesus ascended into heaven after His resurrection — we are living in them; the time-period before Christ returns to establish His kingdom on earth. True to His word, He continues to baptize believers with the Holy Spirit, many with the accompanying manifestation of "tongues" or languages, as initial evidence of baptism.

There have been notable moves of the Holy Spirit in this nation, with the manifestation of "tongues" over the past one hundred or so years, renewing emphasis on that gift of the Holy Spirit — Topeka, Kansas in 1901, Azusa Street in 1906, the Illinois Revivals 1910-1020's and the Charismatic movement in the 1960's, to name a few: Each sweeping across the nation and in some instances further, to other parts of the world. While the manifestation of tongues serves as an initial evidence of Christ's baptism in the Holy Spirit to the believer, it is also a powerful witness to the unbeliever of the power of God, overcoming skepticism: The natural tendency is to fight to retain control of the tongue, which confirms the work of the Holy Spirit when we find we are speaking a language unknown to us.

It is important to remember that the manifestation of the power of God, when and where, and the gifts exercised in the body of Christ are all determined by Christ through the Holy Spirit; He is the administrator —

"Now there are diversities of gifts, but the same Spirit. There are differences of ministries, but the same Lord.

And there are diversities of activities, but it is the same God who works all in all. But the manifestation of the Spirit is given to each one for the profit of all: For to one is given the word of wisdom through the same Spirit, to another the word of knowledge through the same Spirit, to another faith by the same Spirit, to another gifts of healings by the same Spirit, to another the working of miracles by the same Spirit, to another prophecy, to another discerning of spirits, to another different kinds of tongues, to another interpretation of tongues.

But one and the same Spirit works all these things, distributing to each one individually as He wills" (1 Corinthians 12:4-11 emphasis added).

What Is Our Function?

Well, I just threw my first pulpit into a roll-off container, reluctantly, I might add: It is that time in my life to start clearing out the accumulation of "stuff" no longer having value or usefulness. Sundays were regarded a day of rest in our home, so we kids, me age six, and my brothers ages eight and ten, were encouraged to find quiet ways to occupy our time - reading, puzzles, drawing or board games; suppressing the high-energy urge for expression. I guess I regarded Sunday afternoon as a fitting time to preach.

My pulpit was a bookcase that stood forty inches high with three shelves. I used to pull it away from the wall, turn it around and preach to my brothers, both engrossed in whatever they were doing and paying no attention to me. I have no recollection of topics of my sermons, and no idea if my theology was sound, but found the stance, both hands resting on the side of that bookcase, as natural as can be. Though no longer useful as a bookcase, I kept it all these years — a reminder of what I would later realize was part of the gifting my heavenly Father bestowed on me.

That gift took the form of extemporaneous speaking, which was not only used in church but also in my secular job. With no training in public speaking, the Lord enabled me to speak to large groups without notes. As I mentioned earlier, I worked for a German company and remember being asked to address an auditorium of high school students on the importance of studying languages. It was a large auditorium (a Long Island school), I spoke for thirty minutes with a Q and A period at the end. Now if you asked me what I said I couldn't tell you, but the Language teacher was so impressed that in her compliment at the end she commented — *"and without notes".* The same was true of my preaching from the pulpit: The Lord would impress me with a Scripture, and the rest followed. To God be the glory!

The Church of Jesus Christ is the body of Christ, comprised of members from all over the world, with different ages, shapes, color and sizes, past and present. It has one common bond, **Christ Jesus and salvation through Him and Him alone** and one common source of spiritual growth, knowledge and understanding, **the Holy Spirit and the Word of God.** The Church of Jesus Christ in the spiritual realm is perfect, without spot or wrinkle because its members, the body of Christ, are clothed in the righteousness of Christ.

In the natural realm however, the organized church functioning in the world is anything but perfect, mainly because while we are here and part of a church, we are in the process of being conformed to the image of Christ. It is the ongoing work of the Holy Spirit and the struggle between the spirit and the flesh. Paul describes those who walk in darkness, which is who we were before coming to Christ, and then says,

> *"But you have not so learned Christ, if indeed*
> *you have heard Him and have been taught by*
> *Him, as the truth is in Jesus: That you put off,*
> *concerning your former conduct, the old man*
> *which grows corrupt according to the deceitful*
> *lusts, and be renewed in the spirit of your*

*mind, and that you put on the new man **which***
was created according to God in
righteousness and true holiness" (Ephesians 4:20-
24 - emphasis added).

We see this played out in the organized church today, in the same way it was evidenced in the early church - contentions and divisions, selfish ambition - men acting as "mere men."

True to the old nature of man, in many instances man has taken the knowledge the Father has given him through Christ, the eternal word of God, and created his own concept of "church" which I call the organized church. The organized churches have their own identity, rules and regulations, doctrine and hierarchy, always careful to use the Scriptures to support the respective position but ignoring the full counsel of God.

The wonder of God is, that despite our shortcomings and imperfection in our representation of Christ Jesus to the world as His body, He continues to accomplish His plan and purpose. So, we are encouraged to look through eyes of faith at each other and at the church, seeing the finished work, perfect, without spot or wrinkle — because as believers (the body of Christ) we are "in Christ" and He is perfect! We are covered by His righteousness!

The imperfection is visible to the world however, playing into the hand of the enemy of Christ, causing skepticism and criticism; or worse, an excuse for those looking to justify their resistance to the Gospel. Our place individually is to allow Christ to be all that He is and purposes we should be, in Him; allowing His life expression in the way we live, that those we encounter might be drawn to Him.

Gifting

Paul presents an interesting illustration of the functioning body of Christ, comparing it to the human body (1 Corinthians 12:12-31). Like the human body, each member of the body of Christ has a function. Allowing the Word of God to speak for itself, we find a structure for establishing the Church, the foundation being Christ, with gifting provisions to preserve it with continuity.

Reading from 1 Corinthians 12:27,28 - bear in mind that with the ascension of Christ, those appointed to various functions relied upon the Holy Spirit to convey the Word of God. Apart from the Old Testament scrolls and the letters later written to the churches by the apostles (assuming they were copied and circulated), there was nothing in writing.

"Now you are the body of Christ, and members individually. And God has appointed these in the church: first apostles..." the word "apostle" means "one sent forth"; as I understand the Scriptures, referring to the twelve apostles, each having seen the risen Christ; and later Paul, to whom Christ appeared.

Note the word "first" suggesting an order for establishing the church or assembling of believers. Those appointed apostles were sent forth or sent out taking the gospel or good news that Jesus, the Christ was risen from the dead, and His teachings to the Jews. Later we see Paul, appointed by Christ to take the same gospel with the teachings of Christ and revelations given him by Christ for the Church, focusing on his ministry to the gentiles, but also to the Jews. It was the apostle who established teaching or doctrine and order in the assembly of the saints.

"...*second prophets*..." the word "prophet" means "public expounder", today we would refer to them as preachers — their function in the body of Christ is to publicly expound or declare the Word of God. The Old Testament prophet was told by God what to say or convey to the children of Israel publicly - *"the Lord spoke..."*, in many instances giving the prophet foreknowledge of what God is doing or about to do. That is what I understand to be "prophesy or prophesying", a revelation of something yet to come, fore telling.

The New Testament prophet's function in the early church and today is to publicly declare or expound the good news, the teachings of Christ and the new revelations given the Church by Christ through the apostles. We, unlike the early church, have the complete written Word of God, the Bible, containing all that God has revealed to His Church, that is, all He wants us to know. Having been given that knowledge, the prophet declares it publicly. In fact, I would caution against believing anyone who claims to have a new revelation from God.

There is strong disagreement regarding the role of the prophet in the church today. I have experienced several times when someone has come to "prophesy over me", declaring some future event in my life: To prophesy in this context is to declare the word of God, which **must** come to pass.

Let it suffice to say, those things did not come to pass. In discussion with a strong believer in "prophesying", the response to failed prophesy was *"you miss a few"*. I do believe the Holy Spirit can and does give "a word of wisdom" or a "word of knowledge" to someone regarding another person's life by way of encouragement or confirmation of something the person has received from the Lord: We leave the judgment of those things to Christ.

"...third teachers..." is another of the layered provisions of Christ to edify or build up and equip the body of Christ for the ministry of the church. The teacher by way of instruction examines the word of God, for spiritual understanding and application to the body of Christ, collectively and individually.

What I find fascinating is that one can literally see the structure's design and development in the way this truth is presented; building the church whose foundation is Christ. The apostles would not always be there — we know that all but one was martyred; nor could they be in more than one place at a time. But prophets (preachers), pastors and teachers were and continue to be appointed by the Holy Spirit to carry on dispensing the word, aided by the other gifts *"...after that miracles, then gifts of healings, helps, administrations, varieties of tongues,"* right up to this time in the church age.

We cannot close our eyes to the fact that some of the organized church has moved away from the original design. The functions appointed the **servants** of the Lord by Christ for use in the church through the gifting of the Holy Spirit have over time become titled positions of varying degrees of importance. According to God's Word, we are simply servants with a function to perform, our Father showing no partiality — no one person being more important than another in the body of Christ. While we respect one another, and the gifting given by the Spirit of God, we do not elevate one person over another in importance in true Christianity.

Having said that, Paul does differentiate in the importance of the use of gifts to the church, comparing the gift of "tongues" as an example, with that of public speaking "the prophet" and of course what he refers to as the better way - which is "love" (1 Corinthians 12:28-31, 13:).

The supernatural signs and wonders that accompanied the apostles sharing the Gospel, were for unbelievers even as they are today throughout the world; that man might believe seeing the power of God manifested by the Holy Spirit. Each of the gifts are still used by the Holy Spirit to accomplish God's plan and purpose, despite teachings that some are no longer relevant: Notwithstanding, there is a time coming when some of the gifts will not be needed — when Christ establishes His kingdom here on earth: The Millennial reign of Christ.

A Fine-Tuned Instrument

It was the war years (WWII) in Schenectady, New York, that I began my schooling. My father was engaged by General Electric, one of many Companies heavily involved in the war effort, necessitating our move from Lyons, New York, where I was born. Those were the years of rationed goods and air raid drills. I was six years old going on seven, a year older than most in my kindergarten class because born in December, I had to wait for the September enrollment the following year.

As I recall, getting me to go to school was a challenge to begin with. The school was within walking distance, so when the class would take its noon break and nap, I would simply leave and walk home. It was in kindergarten that I was introduced to classical music — "Waltz of the Flowers" from Tchaikovsky's "The Nutcracker".[8] I was to be one of four raindrops in the Spring program performed by the class, set to the music of the "Waltz of the Flowers."

Our part was dancing around the flowers, watering them — I think we each had a sprinkling can. Our costumes were made by our mothers. It was a tan shirt, shorts and cap covered with tinsel. Tinsel back then was very thin long strips of aluminum foil, fragile and easily broken; it was commonly used to decorate a Christmas tree. My mother carefully glued the tinsel to the cloth, so I glistened as I walked. I was so excited I ran to school ahead of the family the day of the performance, unaware that my enthusiasm was rendering me a muddy drop of water compared to the other raindrops: Sadly, by the time I got there I lost most of the tinsel — talk about humiliation and tears - an abundance of them. But that's not the point.

I heard music in that classical piece in a way I never heard music before — hearing every instrument, every part blending harmoniously into a melody. It is another of the gifts given me. It has also served as an illustration of what I understand Christ Jesus intends His body to be.

---

[8] The Nutcracker, a two-act ballet choreographed to the score of Piotr Ilyich Tchaikovsky (Op71)

Think of a Symphony Orchestra comprised of more than one hundred players playing 18 to 25 different instruments; each instrument having a different set of notes to play in order to present what the composer heard when he wrote them.

When the conductor steps up on the platform and lifts his baton, he expects to hear each part blended perfectly. Just one instrument out of tune or hitting a wrong note spoils the sound. I can only thank my Father for His patience, when I think of the number of sour notes I must have produced over the years. Would that the body of Christ would learn that we are each one given a gift, an instrument as it were, and a set of notes to follow, that we might produce a heavenly symphony of perfect harmony and unity, in this earthly realm: Thank you Father for eyes of faith!

"So, what is my function in the body of Christ? I am a servant of Christ my Lord, gifted by the Holy Spirit to preach - the function of prophet, to tend - the function of pastor, to feed - the function of teacher, those entrusted to me — to God be the glory! *"What is yours? Do you know and are you filling your place?* These are questions we should ask ourselves. Understanding that we are here for a purpose, *"for such a time as this",* and given a function to be used as the Holy Spirit prompts, for *"the equipping of the saints for the work of the ministry, for the edifying of the body of Christ, till we all come to the unity of the faith and the knowledge of the Son of God, to a perfect man, to the measure of the stature of the fullness of Christ"* (Ephesians 4:12,13).

The Great Commission

The commission Jesus gave His Church as He prepared to return to His exalted place seated at the right hand of the Father, was two-fold.

The first part - to take the Gospel to the uttermost parts of the earth and share it.

The second part - to make disciples or true followers of those who come to Christ for salvation. Discipleship is a continuous act of grace in an individual believer's life. As stated earlier, it is not an option, rather the normal continuation of the work of grace in one born of the Spirit of God. It is the work of the Holy Spirit, developing and encouraging us in the Word of God and in fellowship with one another as the body of Christ,

> "...till we all come to the unity of the faith and the knowledge of the Son of God, to a perfect man, to the measure of the stature of the fullness of Christ;" (Ephesians 4:13).

Surveying the landscape, it appears that the second of the two-fold commission has been neglected for some time. Some of the organized churches have been seduced by a worldly influence, focusing on the cause of man, caving to social pressures with increased attention given to growing numbers and finances. The result is success by worldly standards but a "light gospel" which is not the Gospel at all, leaving many with a shallow experience that will not sustain them because they are not rooted in the Word.

That is not representative of true Christianity. The Church of Jesus Christ transcends denominational and other boundaries created by man. Functioning as God intends His Church to function, there is a burning desire to see souls added to the kingdom. There is also a desire to see those coming to Christ, grow in faith and in the knowledge of Christ, edified and encouraged in fellowship with the body of Christ by the power of the Holy Spirit: A disciple of and in Christ, a mature force for good in their field of influence. That is Christianity at work, the manifestation of the Holy Spirit operating in a world of darkness through the body of Christ.

Chapter Six

Saved from What?

Let's take an excursion and explore the wonder of "salvation" and its meaning in Christianity. *"Father, this terrane appears rugged, but interesting. The rocky places*

tend to hide the path — sometimes difficult to follow as it winds upward. But thank You for leading the way; we ask that You keep our foot from slipping.

Salvation is a transaction of grace through faith, in certain aspects difficult to describe or express in words because it is a spiritual transition and transformation.

I have been privileged to know some wonderful people over the years — genuinely good, kind and thoughtful people. Some are professed Christians, others are not. It has been interesting to observe that those who make no outward profession of faith in Christ Jesus, often outshine those that do: Their acts of kindness, thoughtfulness and generosity seem to come from the heart as simply the right and natural thing to do, as compared to some of the "good works" performed under the umbrella of Christianity.

The crux of true Christianity is the need of salvation through Christ Jesus. People who by nature are good according to the world's standard of goodness, often find it difficult to see that need. *"Saved from what...?"* is the question that often surfaces in a discussion about salvation. Our natural disposition and for that matter, society, resists the idea that man is basically depraved. The world promotes the idea that there is goodness in every man if one digs deep enough to find it. There is also resistance to the notion that there are only two paths in life from which to choose. One leads to eternal life with Christ, the other leads to eternal death, that is spiritual death, cut off from God: It is a place called hell in the

Bible — described as a lake of fire, a place of eternal torment.

That is why the Scriptures caution,

> *"Enter by the narrow gate, for wide is the gate and broad is the way that leads to destruction, and there are many who go in by it. Because narrow is the gate and difficult is the way that leads to life and there are few who find it"* (Matthew 7:13,14).

> *"Strive to enter through the narrow gate, for many, I say to you, will seek to enter and will not be able"* (Luke 13:24).

Good people can confess a belief in God, even attribute creation to Him, while feeling comfortable making Him what they want Him to be rather than acknowledging who He is by His own definition and revelation. There is a great deception working in the world today that says God is a God of love and we are all children of God. That is simply not true according to the Scriptures.

> *"But as many as received Him (Christ), to them He gave the **right to become children of God**, to those who believe in His Name"* (John 1:12 emphasis added).
>
> *"Behold what manner of love the Father has bestowed on us, that we should be called*

*children of God! Therefore, the world does not know us because it did not know Him (Jesus). Beloved, now we are **children of God**, and it has not yet been revealed what we shall be, but we know that when He is revealed, we shall be like Him for we shall see Him as He Is"* (1 John 3:1,2 emphasis added).

Another is, that we will go to heaven as long as we are good and kind in the way we treat other people and coexist in society, what the Scriptures refer to as" works". That too, is not true. It is faith in Christ and Him alone that secures our eternal place with Him in heaven. As a believer in Christ, we are created for good works, but the works do not save us.

There are those, including some Christians, who dismiss the idea that people who reject Christ's offer of salvation, condemn themselves to an eternity of separation from God and eternal torment in hell, because God is a God of love; despite the Bible saying so.

It is true God is a God of Love, in fact **God is love**. But what is glossed over or left out completely is the fact that the same God of love is also holy and righteous, and His righteousness cannot overlook sin. The flood that destroyed all but eight people during the time of Noah and the destruction of Sodom and Gomorrah gives us a glimpse of what the righteous anger of God looks like.

If we believe in the one true God, attested to throughout the Scriptures, then we know that He is holy and righteous, and if He is true to Himself, He must bring judgment on all unrighteousness and ungodliness. That is one of the things we are saved from - the righteous wrath of God which will be poured out on all unrighteousness in His appointed time.

The position of true Christianity regarding salvation is that man is separated from God because of sin in the heart of man — his sin nature passed down through the seed of the man. That sin nature is not just the things we do that society frowns upon or calls "bad" or that pricks our conscience: They are simply the outcropping of our independent nature and rebellion against God's authority. Our self-will and determination, our independent nature, rejecting God's authority — that is what separates us from Him who created us and loves us.

In fact, He loves us so much, that He assumes responsibility for the breach in our relationship to Him, though it was man who moved against God. He sent His Son into the world to be the sacrificial offering or the atonement for sin — placing on Jesus all of mankind's sin, past, present and future.

"...you shall call His name Jesus, for He will save His people from their sin..." (Matthew 1:21).

"For He made Him who knew no sin to be sin for us that we might become the righteousness of God in Him" (2 Corinthians 5:21).

Without Christ we are like anyone else in the world; we are offspring, God's creation, but eternally separated from His life, light and truth, *"...dead in trespasses and sin."* But, when a man comes to Christ, acknowledging that regardless of any natural goodness he is born in sin and needs a savior, then by faith believing and only then, does he become a **child of God**.

The counter part of the naturally good man who has society's stamp of approval for a good and decent life, is the man whose choices in life have made a mess of things. Seeing the destruction or hopelessness of his life he is much more apt to be receptive to the redeeming love of Christ, as the Holy Spirit draws him — since none can come without the Holy Spirit drawing them.

Salvation through the atoning work of the cross of Christ Jesus results in a new creation; a completely new being, with a new spirit and clean heart. Free from God's wrath, sin(s) forgiven and removed, free of the guilt of the past, and free from the power and penalty of sin, we begin a new life "in Christ" with assurance of eternal life with Him - guaranteed. That is the salvation Christianity presents in the gospel message of hope; that Christ Jesus not only died for our sin(s) but is risen from the dead, exercising power over death.

"So, what must we do to be saved?" The answer Paul gave the Philippian jailer was simply, *"Believe on the Lord Jesus Christ, and you will be saved, you and your household"* (Acts 16:31). We are saved by grace through faith; that is God's grace through the faith He gives to believe. There is no pre-soak and wash required, and nothing we can do will make God love us more than He loved us when He *"...gave His only begotten Son, that*

whoever believes in Him shall not perish but have everlasting life" (John 3:16).

I am always a bit taken back when a professing Christian expresses uncertainty about their eternal destination. That tells me there is something missing in the transaction or a disconnect; a lack of teaching or understanding. Salvation is a complete work — there is nothing to be added. It is faith in Christ Jesus and Him alone; believing who He is and what He obtained for us through His death on the cross and His resurrection. The moment we believe we are a new spiritual being — born again by the Spirit of God with assurance of eternal life. An intellectual acknowledgement of Jesus - that is with the mind only, absent repentance or confession of our need, is not salvation.

"How do we know we are saved? Are there signs in our outward appearance?" Perhaps — but it is not necessarily what we see, rather what others see. Remember, we live by faith — it is not what we see but what we know to be true according to God's Word. Our Father has His own ways of confirming the life-changing work that comes of being "in Christ." A change does occur and because it is spiritual it is difficult to describe — it is something the Holy Spirit conveys to our spirit, manifesting itself in a peace of mind and heart unlike anything experienced before, combined with a sense of being cleansed and overall well-being: He has come to establish residence.

When we speak of amazing grace, it is the fact that as a new creation we are "complete" because we are "in Christ." We are all that God intended the first man Adam, to be, and more because Jesus is perfect in every respect, satisfying the righteous requirement of the law perfectly. The thief on the cross next to Jesus, knew nothing of theology and had no time to get his act together, he simply believed in Him.

The true believer in Christ is born of the Spirit, who immediately makes Himself known expecting to be received and acknowledged: Think of it as our home having been prepared, and the one invited to live there is standing in the doorway waiting to be taken in to establish residence. If we find we are living in fear and anxiety or uncertain of our security "in Christ," it is an indication that we are not appropriating what is ours and available to us through the in-dwelling Holy Spirit.

We have only to look to Him, acknowledge Him, depend upon Him, making Him part of our daily lives. He is our Father's provision through Christ to keep, guide and direct us, conforming us to the image of His Son – and all through the Word of God. He is the one who creates a desire in our hearts to know Christ Jesus, and a hunger in our hearts for the Word of God and for fellowship. If we find ourselves living without those desires we need to *"Examine yourselves (ourselves) as to whether you (we) are in the faith"*, as Paul writes to the Corinthians (2 Corinthians 13:5 emphasis added).

There is an expression that circulates throughout Christianity, *"Once saved always saved."* It is a discussion that most circles avoid where there is a difference of opinion. The danger is, creating a false sense of security: It has opened the door to deceptive teaching, suggesting that because Christ Jesus died for all our sin(s), we can do what we want and live as we please with impunity.

There is truth in the statement, but only as it relates to the atoning work of the cross. What Jesus accomplished in giving Himself to be made sin that we might become the righteousness of God, was a finished or complete work, leaving nothing to be added because Jesus did it all; and He did it as a means to restore all of mankind and creation to God the Father — **it cannot be undone, the provision is always there**.

When we hold the statement *"Once saved always saved"* up to the light of the Word of God, we cannot ignore the serious warnings such as that above to *"examine yourself..."* or to *"continue in the faith grounded and steadfast and are not moved away from the hope of the gospel..."* (Colossians 1:23).

> *"...Moses indeed was faithful in all his house as a servant, for a testimony of those things which would be spoken afterwards, but Christ as a Son over His own house,* ***whose house we are if we hold fast the confidence and the rejoicing of the hope firm to the end"*** (Hebrews 3:5,6 emphasis added).

> *"Beware brethren, lest there be in any of you an evil heart of unbelief in departing from the living God; but exhort one another daily, while it is called 'Today,' lest any of you be hardened through the deceitfulness of sin. For we have become partakers of Christ* ***if we hold the beginning of our confidence***

steadfast to the end..." (Hebrews 3:12-14 emphasis added).

While nothing can separate us from the love of God in Christ, we can be moved or walk away from Him by yielding to temptation.

> *"But each one is tempted when he is drawn away by his own desires and enticed. Then, when desire has conceived, it gives birth to sin; and sin, when it is full-grown **brings forth death**"* (James 1:14,15 emphasis added).

The truth is that though we know Christ Jesus, having experienced the atoning work of His cross and His resurrection, we can still be tempted because we live in this corruptible body. If we yield, temptation gives birth to sin. We can at any point run to our Father, confess our sin and ask for and find forgiveness. Oswald Chambers draws a beautiful parallel of this truth to the parable of the Lost Son. If we continue to live in habitual sin, we have separated ourselves, no longer walking in the light, rather walking in darkness, which will ultimately lead to spiritual death.

"Is there a way back?" Yes, thank the Lord, but it is no longer the way of repentance (Hebrews 6:4-6). To **repent**, or **repentance**, is the change of mind that occurs when we are drawn by the Spirit of God and exposed to the Word of God - the Gospel, the message of hope and salvation. Once having received the gift of salvation, and lured away

by natural desires, the way back is by **confession** of sin - but that is a field trip for another day.

So, having by faith received Christ and the atoning work of the cross — we are complete, as was the thief that hung on the cross next to Jesus. He died and his soul and spirit were immediately ushered into the presence of the living God, or as Jesus said to him, *"...today you will be with Me in Paradise"*. With no time to study theology the thief having acknowledged his sin, met every aspect of God's righteous requirement because he believed in Christ and was clothed in His righteousness. That is salvation!

Should a person be given years to live following salvation, then comes the opportunity to become a disciple of Christ Jesus, appropriating all the Father has provided for life here, in Christ, through the Holy Spirit.

Discipleship

If you have ever committed yourself to follow anything requiring diligence and dedication, whether it be body building, playing an instrument or an ideology, you became a "disciple". Discipleship is to follow something or someone and pursue that interest or follow that teaching - to give yourself completely to that pursuit. In Christianity, it is "to know Christ" that becomes the goal in life. The apostle Paul articulates the principle in Philippians 3:7-14: *"But indeed I count all things loss for the excellence of the knowledge of Christ Jesus my Lord......that I may gain Christ and be found in Him...that I may know Him and the power of His resurrection, and the fellowship of His sufferings..."*

(Philippians 3:8,9,910).

I understand discipleship to be an intended extension of salvation, not an option. The commission Christ Jesus gave His Church involved sharing the gospel that souls would be added to the kingdom and then, having come to Christ, making them disciples of Him. That work in a believer is the Holy Spirit's work in tandem with and in the body of Christ, to instruct and encourage a new believer in the Word of God. That through fellowship in the Word, they become firmly rooted in the faith and strengthened in the inner man; continuing to grow in grace and in the knowledge of the Lord Jesus Christ. That describes the function of the Church as our Lord intends it should function, vital for the child of God.

The reason discipleship is not an option is expressed by Paul writing to the Corinthians:

> *"...do you not know that your body is the temple of the Holy Spirit who is in you, whom you have from God, you are not your own? You were bought at a price; therefore, glorify God in your body and in your spirit, which are God's"* (1 Corinthians 6:19,20).

These words also give added meaning to the parable Jesus used, i.e., like the builder who sits down and counts the cost, before starting to build. (Luke 14:28). While salvation is a gift, it is none-the-less a transaction. Coming to Christ, we are no longer our own and need the Holy Spirit's help to grow into and remain steadfast in that truth. We tend to read the words but slide over the meaning.

This should be a living reality in our lives and in our churches. Sadly, some of the organized churches naming the name of our Lord Jesus Christ, have lost sight of their purpose. It appears that the Holy Spirit has been replaced by organization, theater and programs designed to appeal: It is as if we have learned how to "have church" without Him. In other cases, form and ceremony following tradition leave no room for the free expression of the Holy Spirit in ministry. The result can be stifling, *"...having a form of godliness but denying the power..."*; leaving a people who claim to have experienced the grace of God through salvation, but whose lives fail to bear witness by the inner workings of the Holy Spirit. It cannot be emphasized enough, that an encounter with the Christ of Calvary is a life-changing experience in true Christianity.

We look at our natural children and follow their development in stages, expecting them to grow: They move from milk to solid foods as bones and muscles develop. They begin to scurry around on all fours until that day comes when they begin to walk. Finding the ability to get around on their own, they are into everything because of curiosity — wanting to know. Why would we think our heavenly Father would care less about His children's development; He doesn't! That is why He has made provision for everything we need, in Christ, through the effective work of the Holy Spirit and the body of Christ.

"What do we do when we encounter a "Christian" who shows no signs of change or growth?" Condemn them?

No, we are encouraged to pray for them, love them and come alongside them, drawing them into fellowship in the Word of God, if they will: The Holy Spirit working through the Word will convince, correct and change them. It can be a slow process requiring love and patience, each person being different but intimately known by the Holy Spirit. What a joy to see them firmly rooted and grounded in the Word - a true disciple of Christ Jesus, to God be the glory!

"Why is this aspect of Christianity so important?" Consider the example given by the nation Israel: the other nations witnessed God's power on behalf of the Israelites who were God's chosen people: Israel was intended to be a light to the other nations. But to the contrary, through their disobedience turning to other gods, they brought reproach causing the other nations to blaspheme His name.

In truth, the old excuse *"I'm only human"* used so often to cover our failures, doesn't hold water because we are a new creation in Christ and have been given the Holy Spirit. Our lives are to be a living testimony of the transforming power of a living God, to those around us — a light in darkness; that those we encounter would see something of Christ Jesus and be drawn to Him. The light is Christ! *"...Christ in you, the hope of glory..."* the indwelling Holy Spirit conforming us to the image of Christ.

We cannot begin to imagine what took place in that heavenly boardroom when the three of them, Father, Son and Holy Spirit, laid out the plan of salvation before the foundation of the world. What we do know is that it is wonderful, the answer to all of man's troubles and woes.

So, when you hear the question *"...saved from what?"* have a ready answer, *"I am a sinner saved by grace..."* from sin, from the wrath of God and the sting of death. The fact that God loved us and chose us before the foundation of the world is, in and of itself, amazing. We contributed nothing. He did it all through His Son; the atoning work of the cross and the resurrection of Jesus, from the dead.

The invitation is, come as you are — right now — it is not a white tie and tails occasion, you don't have to clean yourself up or bring a dish to pass to be accepted. That is salvation; our Father's perfect, once and forever plan of redemption and reconciliation accomplished through Christ Jesus and His cross. We are saved by grace through faith, that is, by believing in and on Christ and Him alone!

Chapter Seven

Lobster Anyone?

Exploring the wonder of Christianity is not limited to enjoying lazy days on grassy slopes or meandering through lovely meadows. A field trip may also take us to places that sharpen our sensitivity to the harsh realities of the dangers of the influence of the world around us, as I expect this one may.

Now I have never prepared lobster for anyone, although I have enjoyed it on many occasions. I am told that the lobster must be alive when it is cooked, so it is placed in a pot of water which is then slowly heated - the lobster totally unaware of its peril. That reminds me of sin and the subtlety of the enemy of man's soul — "...*You will not surely die, for God knows in the day you eat of it, your eyes will be opened, and you will be like God, knowing good and evil"* (Genesis 3:4,5).

Sin is a subject most would rather avoid but is the source of man's separation from His creator and all the problems with which man has had to cope since Adam's transgression. Before the Law, God gave Adam a command which Adam chose to disobey: And so, it was that evil entered the heart of man and the Garden of Eden, disturbing the perfect order established by the Creator — we know what happened as a result.

In the accounts recorded in the Scriptures the next evidence of evil is revealed in the heart of Cain. This too before the Law, but not without knowledge — Cain having the knowledge of both good and evil. He chose evil, despite God's warning that sin was at his door desiring to have control of him: He killed his brother Abel.

Over the course of time, displays of God's righteous anger toward the wickedness of man reveals His hatred of sin: **Enter the Law**. The Ten Commandments were given, not to save us but to instruct or teach us regarding sin. It would be a wonderful world if everyone lived by the saying *"let your conscience be your guide"* — that is assuming everyone would choose to do good rather than evil. But having knowledge of good and evil did and does not change the heart of man so the law came so man would know when he broke it - identifying sin.

If the road sign says 55 mph, and I am driving 62 mph — I am breaking the law. I can rationalize and justify my lawless action because I know that generally speaking, law enforcement won't pull me over unless I exceed 62 mph. But that does not change the fact that I am a law breaker. In giving the Ten Commandments, God knew that man was incapable of keeping every one of them; and failing in one only, makes us a law breaker, a sinner: **Enter Christ Jesus**.

Alright, I know what you are thinking — *"what does any of this have to do with cooking lobsters and*

Christianity?" As a Christian, we know that the world *"lies in the sway of the wicked one"*, that is, under the control and influence of Satan. Many people are caught up in their own world unconcerned about "sin"; so, we shouldn't be surprised by the conduct of those in the world who are without Christ. Jesus said He did not come to condemn the world because the world is condemned already - He came to save it. Jesus satisfied the righteous requirements of the law perfectly for us since we were incapable of keeping it. So here we are, safe "in Christ" through salvation. But the harsh reality is, sin still lurks in the shadows looking for opportunity to catch us off guard.

The depth of this truth suddenly struck me one day, giving birth to the following poem, revealing what I was delivered from, in Christ –

I Dare Not Trust Myself

By David Buisch
9 November 1996

Lord, thank you for the quiet times,
for Your love revealing
hidden darkness still within which
I would keep concealing.

I see beneath the thin veneer of natural love and
grace, motivation ill-begot among which is the
trace of jealousy, of greed and pride,
whose works though covered well,
bring forth the same destruction as
the day when Adam fell.

Wickedness, perversity in deep recesses hide though
inoffensive to the world as "just my darker side".
Your Word and gentle Spirit exposes to the light,
propensity for evil deeds as black as darkest night.

What help, what hope is there for me -
what hope for anyone,
left to self-help remedies; for when the day is
done communing with one's inner
self, self-love and satisfaction,
does naught to curb my appetite for
my self-centered action.

Well said "I am a sinner", redeemed by love and
grace revealed in truth and righteousness
which cannot be erased.
For You are, have always been, and will forever be, the
same unchanging architect of this soul's destiny.

You are my help when left to choose,
my Lord and constant source:
I dare not trust myself in life, so You direct my course.

In Christ, we are free of the power of sin, but not free
from temptation and Satan never gives up in his attempts
to destroy the work of God. We live in this corruptible
body, exposing us to its desires and demands; thoughts
that draw our attention to those desires and past
appetites.

The enemy of our soul seizes on the opportunity to capture our thought; *"after all just this once won't hurt anyone."* All the time the Holy Spirit is quietly saying - don't go there, it is a trap. *"Well, the sky didn't fall - didn't get a thump on the head - so, just one more time."* — and like the lobster in the pot of water unaware it is being cooked, that particular desire takes hold, subtly and quietly — and here is the danger: Each time we yield, the easier it gets to yield and eventually without pangs of conscience. We plug our ears to the Spirit's prompting and warnings. James describes the process:

> *"Let no one say when he is tempted, 'I am tempted by God'; for God cannot be tempted by evil, nor does He Himself tempt anyone. But each one is tempted when he is drawn away by his own desires and enticed. Then, when desire has conceived, it gives birth to sin, and sin, when it is fully grown brings forth death"* (James 1:13-15).

"If, as a Christian, I am then overcome by sin, is it the Holy Spirit's fault - He failed to keep me from stumbling? No, regardless of the nature of the temptation or trial, God always provides a way of escape. If we listen to the Holy Spirit, if we do not rebuff Him and His counsel and the Word of God, we will be kept from falling or stumbling. But we are apt to do to the Holy Spirit what I used to do when I was living in sin: in response to my

mother's attempt to warn me I used to say to myself, under my breath -*"I hear you but I am not listening."*

One of the "wiles" of the enemy of our souls is the subtle use of temptation to separate us from fellowship and the safeguards the body of Christ provides. I remember early in my "Christian" experience — living in New York City, fresh out of the Navy and attending Glad Tidings Tabernacle, an Assemblies of God church in Manhattan pastored by Marie Brown. I lived at the YMCA while looking for work as an artist. Through a casual conversation I met a young Jewish man also living at the "Y" and had opportunity to witness to him about Jesus. I befriended him and eventually invited him to church.

I think it was after the second occasion he attended church with me that he said it was my turn to go somewhere with him. The short of a long story is that over time he was not responding to his exposure to the Word of God, but I was responding to the allure of the world to which he had exposed me; art, theater and ballet — I found it all fascinating. I had taken a job to have income and moved to an apartment on Manhattan's West side. I began to make friends outside Christian fellowship; some were notable in the world of theater. My attendance in church eventually dropped off to the extent that the pastor called my mother to know where I was and if I was all right.

"How did it happen?" Well, there is much more to the story but let it suffice to say that it was a subtle, gradual move away from the Lord — like the lobster in the pot of water, I didn't realize what was happening. Nothing

happened that caused me to turn away; I had not been offended or wounded by the church. It was a slow but gradual alienation of my affection, aided by curiosity and rationalization that there was nothing wrong in enjoying my new-found interests. If you asked me if I was a Christian I would say, *"yes!"*

It was not the lack of proper teaching. To the contrary, in my eighty-three years, I have never known a better pastor. The life of Marie Brown and her ministry is a wonderful testimony of God's grace, an example of godliness, complete dedication and faithfulness with a true pastor's heart; filled with the Holy Spirit, a prayer warrior and faithful minister of the Word of God.

What it revealed was my immaturity, and vulnerability: Having head knowledge but lacking heart knowledge that comes from being grounded in the Word of God. My life became more and more influenced by friends outside the faith. Since some were associated with the theater and ballet, they were essentially night people. To maintain their friendship, I began burning the candle at both ends and ended up in the hospital in critical condition.

It was my mother and Marie Brown who were wakened at three in the morning, sensing the urgent need to pray for me. That was the same time intense fever threatened my life as I lay in the Lexington Avenue Hospital. Neither of them knew I was in the hospital, but the urgency impressed upon them by the Holy Spirit was such that Marie Brown called my mother. Both prayer warriors, they continued in prayer until released, not knowing what was happening.

All I remember was the night in the hospital I woke up, my whole body burning with fever. According to the Company physician I was in a coma for three days before the fever broke. His report to my employer was, they were not certain I would live and expected that If I did, there would be severe brain damage: But God! So complete was God's intervention, that I was back to work within a week.

Now, you would think that that experience alone would wake me up. It did not, but God is faithful and knows those that are His. His ways are indeed past finding out. It would be some time later that the Holy Spirit enabled me to see my life and how far I had drifted, or for a better word, fallen from grace. Like the lobster in boiling water, I was unaware that I was spiritually dying.

"*Is there a way back?* As mentioned in Chapter 6, there is always a way back because what Christ Jesus did for us cannot be undone - but no longer by way of repentance (Hebrews 6:4-6).

Oswald Chambers,[9] draws a parallel to this truth in his comments on the parable of the Lost Son (Luke 15:11-32). If you remember, the youngest of two sons approaches his father and asks for his inheritance. He takes it and leaves home squandering what he received in loose living. When he comes to the end of his resources, he finds himself hungry and living in squalor and remembers that his father's servants had a better life than his — so he returns home.

---

[9] The Complete Works of Oswald Chambers ©2000 by Oswald Chambers Publications Association, Limited. All rights reserved.

The way back, "coming home" is by way of confession of sin, seeking forgiveness — *"Father, I have sinned **against heaven** and in your sight, and I am no longer worthy to be called your son."* (Luke 15:21 emphasis added) The father's response was, *"...for this my son **was dead** and is alive again; he was lost and is found."*

When King David sinned by taking Uriah's wife Bathsheba, and then arranging the death of her husband Uriah, to cover his sin, it was the Lord through the prophet Nathan, that exposed it. David's response was, *"I have sinned **against the Lord**"* (2 Samuel 12:13 emphasis added). It was not against Uriah or Bathsheba, but against the Lord. The truth is, since sin no longer has power over us, our yielding to the temptation to sin is deliberate, creating separation from fellowship with our Father in Christ: Restoration can only come by seeking forgiveness for trampling our Father's grace and the blood of Christ under foot. It is by way of confession of our sin against Him — *"If we confess our sins, He is faithful and just to forgive our sins and to cleanse us from all unrighteousness"* (1 John 1:9).

Paul addresses this problem in his letter to the Romans, chapter 7. His soliloquy relating his experience is not offering a Christian an excuse for failures in the flesh — like the once popular comedian's saying, *"the devil made me do it".* Rather he is illustrating the struggle between his flesh which is dead and his spirit which is alive in Christ. As a Christian, a new creation in Christ, our flesh or "old nature" through the body of flesh is always there to be used by the enemy of our souls to trip us in our walk of faith:

"Therefore, let him who thinks he stands take heed lest he fall. No temptation has overtaken you except such as is common to man; but God is faithful, who will not allow you to be tempted beyond what you are able, but with the temptation will also make the way of escape, that you may be able to bear it" (1 Corinthians 10:12,13).

Hattie Hammond, an ordained Assemblies of God minister, was a much sought-after speaker in her day. The focus of her ministry was the work of the Holy Spirit with emphasis on total commitment to Christ. I was privileged to hear her speak on several occasions: Addressing an assembly, she used to say, *"...we think we can handle sin, but we can't."* There are no truer words spoken.

If you are a Christian reading this and know what it is to feel spiritually listless — that dead zone, you cannot pray and have a sense of being cut off from God and the body of Christ; recognize it as a warning sign. That is one of the effects of unconfessed sin and the enemy of our souls looks for that opportunity to isolate us — like the lioness singling out her prey from the herd. The "accuser of the brethren" is right there to whisper in our ear, *"and you call yourself a Christian!"*. That is the time to run to our Father; clear out whatever stands in the way of our communion with Him in Christ and fellowship in the body of Christ. Remember, the lobster never realizes it is being cooked — to death.

There is not one in the body of Christ who is exempt from temptation. That is why we are instructed to be alert, and why Paul writes to the Galatians, *"Brethren, if a man is overtaken in any trespass, you who are spiritual restore such a one in a spirit of gentleness, considering yourself lest you also be tempted"* (Galatians 6:1).

Chapter Eight

Worship

*"God is Spirit and those who worship Him must worship **in spirit** and **truth**"* (John 4:24).

I know a lovely spot that overlooks Lake Ontario. The view from the top of the bluff provides a wide-angle panorama, a sense of limitless expanse. On certain days the blue of the sky erases the horizon — the blue hue of the water and the sky blending, becoming one - the wonder of God's limitless expanse and a perfect field trip.

We find the quotation above in John's gospel, Chapter 4: Jesus speaking to the Samaritan woman at Jacob's well.

"How do we worship an invisible God who exists in everything?" Perhaps a good place to start is to acknowledge that He does exist in everything and that everything exists **for His pleasure**. The tendency of man is to think of himself as the center of the universe - god of his own little world. If we concern ourselves with truth, we come to know as Christians, that it is not about us, rather about Christ Jesus: Pleasing the Father through our position "in Christ", through whom the Father is working and in whom He is well pleased.

The focus of true Christianity is Jesus Christ — exalting Him, with praise and worship of Him in **everything**, because it pleases our Father. Sadly, many "Christians" today, view worship as the fifteen to twenty minutes spent in a Sunday morning church service, singing the choruses and songs or hymns **we like** regardless of the message the words convey. If we would take time to examine the words with discernment, we would see that too often they are about us, we are the focus rather than exalting Christ.

Like too many things today, that form of worship, generally speaking, has been so organized that there is no room for the Holy Spirit to minister: The worst of it is the rationalization - that whatever we offer up to God is acceptable to Him *"because He knows my heart"*; and He does and knows how easily we deceive ourselves.

In contrast, some of the sweetest memories I have as a Christian, is the presence of the Holy Spirit hovering over a body of believers caught up in true worship in spirit: Words of praise, the name of Jesus exalted, all rising in beautiful, heavenly orchestrated harmony, no prescribed lyrics and free of time constraints. Here is a rabbit trail we should follow -

Make a Joyful Noise

I started playing the piano or rather tinkering with it, when I was four or five years old. After the war, my family moved to Geneva, New York, to a house on Seneca Lake. My mom recognized that I had a natural gift and ear for music, so she arranged for piano lessons with the music professor at Hobart College on Saturdays, in exchange for house cleaning; he was a bachelor. He lived two houses away from us on the lake, so it was convenient: I was nine or ten years old.

I don't recall the professor's name, but I remember him. Looking back, I realize he was not accustomed to dealing with children, let alone one as sensitive as I apparently was. He was pleasant, but all business. He had a beautiful grand piano and sat me down asking me to play something for him on my first visit. I don't recall what I played, but it would have been something I picked out by ear, which I played with difficulty because the keyboard was tight. He immediately started me with scales and introduced me to the first sheet of music from a beginner's lesson book. He played it for me and sent me home to practice for the following week.

I returned the following week and played it perfectly for him. He was pleased and proceeded to the next piece, played it for me and sent me home to practice for the following week - of course, practicing the scales as well. I returned, the third week of my lessons, and played both assigned pieces perfectly. But this week he did something different, after exercises in the scales, he pointed to the next sheet of music and told me to practice it for the following week.

Need I tell you, the following week he was not pleased at all as I struggled to find the notes. *"You have not been reading the notes - you're playing by ear. I don't have time for this!"* He slammed the keyboard cover down, barely missing my hands and sent me home in tears. Though that ended my piano lessons, it did not dampen my love for music.

In our Father's good time, He gifted me with the ability to play the piano and organ, contributing to worship for forty plus years. All this to say the gifting of God is marvelous.

Joyful Noise

"Make a joyful noise...". A cacophony of sound is not what the Psalmist had in mind when he used the word "noise": Rather the unison of voices and instruments, in a joyful shout or song.

Now, stop and think for a moment about church music: Some of it has endured for centuries. There are the contributions of the great music masters who used their gift to create Sonatas, Preludes and Requiems to glorify God. They are magnificent, lofty orchestral and choral pieces that are still used today: The well-known Handel's "Messiah" is just one example.

But what of the admonition to be *"...filled with the Spirit, speaking to one another in psalms and hymns and spiritual songs, singing and making melody in your heart to the Lord..."*(Ephesians 5:18,19) — the offering of praise and worship by the individual or collective members of the body of Christ. I went through a period when the Lord gave me a number of songs, both words and music.

Here are the words to one that illustrates the above:

Let Everything with Breath Praise the Lord

By David Buisch - 6 November 1981
(Based on the 150th Psalm)

Oh, praise ye the Lord, yes,
praise Him all ye lands.
Praise Him with your voices,
praise Him with your hands.
Praise Him for His greatness,
praise Him for His might.
Praise and glorify Him for
His truth and light!

Praise Him with the trumpet,
make a mighty sound.

Praise Him with the psaltery,
let your praise abound!
Praise Him with the harp, the
timbrel and the dance.
Praise and glorify Him in
every circumstance!

Oh, praise ye the Lord, with
strings and organ too.
Praise Him from your heart
in everything you do!
Praise Him with the cymbals,
praise in one accord.
Let everything with breath
Praise the Lord!

What did the psalmist mean when he wrote,"...come, magnify the Lord with me" (Psalm 43:3)? During my years of pastoring, we periodically invited the saints from other churches to join us for an evening "Songfest", a time of worship and praise, followed by a time of fellowship. Hearing all those voices magnifying the Lord together gave me goose bumps.

Find an "old" hymnal and thumb through it - listen to some of the words. So much of the music was written to magnify the Lord. You will find hymns of praise, hymns of faith, some bearing witness to the grace of God, His glorious salvation through Christ Jesus and His precious blood. There are victorious songs, joyful songs, and simple choruses, focusing on the majesty, holiness and faithfulness of God our Father and our Lord Jesus Christ.

Are all the words scriptural? Are all inspired by the Holy Spirit? Not necessarily: They sometimes reveal the spiritual maturity of the composer or lack thereof; where the composer was in his walk of faith when the words were penned. This is where the church should exercise discernment, always aware that our worship is, or should be an **offering to God** and as such **must** be in spirit and truth. Sadly, this is where much of the organized church has failed.

We seem to have a natural tendency to turn things around. Here our Father has done everything through His Son to reconcile us to Himself. He has provided everything we need "in Christ" and by the power of His Holy Spirit, to live a godly life fully pleasing to Him. And yet much of our "Christian" music suggests He must do more, when what is lacking is in our response to His word, obedience and submission. One contemporary song offered as worship actually contained the phrase, "keep me if You can."

The music of the world has always been a source of entertainment. The lyrics of most songs focus on man, his passion, joy, and troubles. It is an art form that is addictive, and never more so than through today's technology — people plugged in to constant noise. Like Christian music, it has gone through various forms of expression, influenced by various cultures, but none like the current trend.

Until recent years, there has remained a reverence for what I would call sacred music, even though there are different styles of expression. The "gospel music sound", which is a unique style of music, is said to be the inspiration of Thomas Dorsey who introduced the influence of the "Blues" in Christian music. It is very much a part of the expression of worship in many churches today. There are other styles, but in recent years there has been a significant infiltration of the world's music in the church unlike any other time in the history of the church — by that I mean the deafening sound and throbbing beat.

Despite knowing that God will not accept as sacred things tainted by the profane, the church has invited the music of the world to appeal to a younger generation, albeit music with "Christian" lyrics: Which is not to say all contemporary Christian music falls into that category. This is the day of "rock bands" which dominate most of the popular music world. In the church the result is worship, for the most part absent the Spirit of God. Without the Holy Spirit, the children of God are robbed of the blessing of worship in spirit and truth through music and words which are uplifting, encouraging, victorious and joyful, an offering from a heart of thanksgiving.

"Is it possible to work up a spiritual frenzy through music? — Yes, but we should be asking, *"what spirit?"* There is a difference between spirit worship and soul worship. True "worship" in Christianity is more than music! If we believe the Word of God, we know and understand that we are no longer our own; our bodies have become the temple of the Holy Spirit, *"...therefore glorify God **in your body and in your spirit which are God's**"* (1 Corinthians 6:19 emphasis added). To glorify God is to magnify and worship Christ Jesus — in doing so, pleasing our Father.

"How do we do that in everything?" Through consciousness that we are indwelt by the Spirit of God and depend upon Him for the enabling power. Be *"filled with the Holy Spirit"* who works through the Word of God to conform us to the image of Christ Jesus, transforming our minds, our attitudes and way of thinking. Our Father desires that our daily lives give life to the words, *"...giving thanks always **for all things** to God the Father in the name of our Lord Jesus Christ..."* (Ephesians 5:20 emphasis added); that He be glorified.

Unpacking the truth of God's Word is like drawing a picture of something by connecting dots; until we connect them the picture is incomplete. We read the Scriptures or listen to them being read but much of what we read and hear doesn't enter or stay in our consciousness — "in one ear and out the other" — we don't connect the dots. We read that through the atoning work of the cross of Jesus, we are a new creation born of the Spirit of God and have become one with the Father in Christ. We understand, at least intellectually, that God is holy — but fail to connect that with the admonition, "...be holy...". Why? Because we are in Christ.

I have often asked why it takes so long to realize that the words, "...and you are not your own...", gives our Father the right to do with us who are in Christ, as He pleases. So, whether we walk through the valley of the shadow of death, or He leads us beside the still water, He is one and the same Shepherd. When we connect the dots, we see that everything the Father has done and is doing through Christ, is for His glory and according to His perfect plan and purpose. When we pray "...never-the-less, Your will be done..." and mean it, that too is worship.

The perfect example of that truth is Christ Jesus, Himself. We also see that truth lived out in the life of the apostle Paul. Oswald Chambers,[5] who at the young age of forty-three, suffering from complications of an emergency appendectomy, refused a hospital bed that could otherwise be used to attend a wounded soldier. He connected the dots, understanding that if it was His Father's will, he would live and if not, he would physically die yet he would live — he died physically but lives eternally.

As Christians, our response to the situations of life are opportunities to worship: Responding by faith, joyfully with patience and perseverance in word and in deed, is worship. It is often in severe testing that the life of Christ in us becomes most evident. "...Your will be done" — is an expression of faith in Christ and Him alone. The Scriptures tell us that,

> "...we are His workmanship, created in Christ Jesus for **good works, which God prepared beforehand** that we should walk in them"
> (Ephesians 2:10 emphasis added).

> That we, "...may have a walk worthy of the Lord, fully pleasing Him, **being fruitful in every good work** and increasing in the knowledge of God; strengthened with all might accord to His glorious power, for all patience and longsuffering with joy; giving thanks to the Father who has qualified us to be partakers of the inheritance of the saints in the Light" (Colossians 1:10-12 emphasis added).

> "Let your light so shine before men, that they may see your good works and glorify your Father which is in heaven" (Matthew 5:16).

Doing all for the glory of God. This too is worship! This truth inspired a poem - "Are You the One":

Are You the One?

By David Buisch - 16 February 1996

My love I've not withheld from any longing for My touch. My
life I freely gave because My Father loved so much.

It grieves Me when I look around and see life's poverty; the
ones deprived of peace and joy, which they would find in Me.

Lacking love and grace with which to face the trials of life, I
see them broken, fettered in a world that's torn by strife.

Is there one who know My love, who has some time to spare?
One who knows My peace and joy - tell them that I care.

You who know My comfort, know My strength and
faithfulness, take a moment, share My love with one who's
in distress.

The lonely hearts with faces etched with pain, despair and loss,
need to know I bore their pain and sorrow on the cross.

Tell them that My loving arms extended on that tree long
to hold and comfort them and set the captive free.

To the shut-in, sick and helpless, all those stripped of dignity,
imprisoned by their bodies, who will speak to them for Me?

Are you the one with words of hope, the one they're waiting for?
To know my saving grace and love both now and evermore.

If you're Mine and know My love, take some time to show it. By
your words and deeds of love other too can know it.

Chapter Nine

What a Nut!

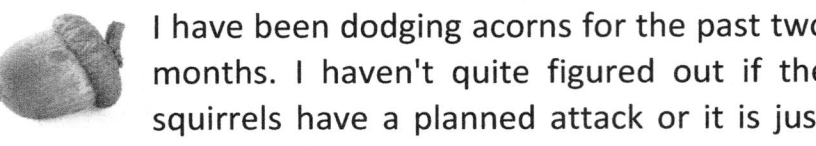 I have been dodging acorns for the past two months. I haven't quite figured out if the squirrels have a planned attack or it is just random hits. They are up there in this beautiful oak tree my father transplanted years ago, dropping acorns — from the force, it seems more like they are being thrown.

In addition to the squirrels, I have a chipmunk companion who apparently lives with me. I say this because I have found as many as eight acorns hidden under my pillow, five in my shoe and four next to my desk top computer. Just yesterday when making up the bed I found two acorns on the comforter.

When I was fifteen years old, my parents bought a piece of property in upstate New York, called an island. It was two hundred thirty acres surrounded by water; woodland, some tillable land and marshes. During the summer months I spent a lot of time exploring what we called the "back forty" — forty acres completely wooded and bordered by Beaver Creek, Blind Creek and Lake

Ontario. It is a wonderful place for field trips and reflection.

Blind Creek is an isolated body of water, separated from Lake Ontario by a barrier bar which in years long past would break through the gravel bar in the Spring and empty into the Lake.

Photo: *Blind Creek, Huron, New York*

At one of the most southerly points there was a massive oak tree, which still stands. Thought to be well over two hundred years old then - sixty plus years ago, it has withstood the severe weather fronts that sweep across Lake Ontario all year long over those many years. Looking at it, it is hard to imagine that it grew from an acorn.

Now, if you have never seen an acorn planting itself, it is fascinating to see how our Creator has engineered this little nut. The first signs of growth are from the top of the acorn which has shed the cap and cracked enough to send a taproot straight down into the soil — like a spike. It is that taproot that continues to penetrate the earth pushing downward, further and further with offshoots that ultimately form the root network that makes the mighty oak what it is.

It reminds me of God's design for the life of a child of His. When we come to Christ Jesus, a new creation born of the Spirit of God, the first sign of life is the taproot — Christ Himself, the Word of the living God — we find ourselves "in Christ". He is the Word by design, intended to feed and nourish the life as it grows to maturity, straight up, but grounded and deeply rooted.

There is another oak tree that I planted when I was seventeen. It was a sapling probably eighteen inches high. I brought it back from the woods and asked my Dad if I could plant it in the back yard. He consented and gave me instructions,

"Be sure you dig a hole deep enough to accommodate the roots" (They were probably two feet long with offshoots). He continued, *"Fill the hole with water and be sure you have enough room to spread the roots out as you put the soil back around them."*

Well, you can imagine at that age I just wanted to get it planted. I didn't dig the hole deep enough and I didn't spread the roots out enough. The result some sixty-five years later is a squat oak tree with a massive trunk for its age: a wonderful climbing tree, but far from the image of a stately, mighty oak.

Knowledge of Christ through the Word of God imparted by the Spirit of God is the most important and significant aspect of our walk of faith in this new life we have in Christ, along with good Christian fellowship. He is our life, the root upon which we depend for spiritual growth. Sadly, for so many, it is this aspect which is most neglected. The enemy of our souls in his cunning and devious ways has introduced alternatives through the good intentions of those who offer short cuts or a — "something is better than nothing" — approach.

To say it simply, there is nothing, no substitute for time spent with the Holy Spirit in the Word of God. Prayerfully approaching the Word, asking for wisdom, spiritual understanding, ruminating, meditating on it until it nourishes the soul. *"Be diligent (study} to present yourself approved to God, a worker who does not need to be ashamed, rightly dividing the word of truth..."* (2 Timothy 2:15 emphasis added). When we are grounded and rooted in the word of God, deeply rooted like the oak, we are less likely to be fooled or caught off guard by the wiles of the enemy. In the same way the oak tree withstands the storms that assail it, we are enabled to stand in the face of adversity and the trials and temptations of life.

There is an overwhelming amount of printed material and visual aids in the marketplace dealing with Christianity. Most of it is good, inspirational, instructive and encouraging, but none of it replaces the value of time spent **reading** the Word with a desire to **know** and **understand**. There are helps that structure daily reading to read through the Bible in a year; that is constructive. There are daily devotions that provide a thought for the day based on a certain verse or portion of Scripture, and they are good; but the reward of a quiet time with the Holy Spirit in the Word of God, is far greater.

Reading this book is good, but I pray it is not only good and easy reading but effective in helping the reader understand that it cannot replace the wisdom and knowledge the Spirit of God wishes to impart directly through the Word of God. It takes time and may require a sacrifice of time but that is how the Christian grows, reading slowly, meditating, acknowledging dependence on the Holy Spirit; allowing the Spirit of God to give us knowledge with spiritual understanding. He takes the head knowledge of truths acquired by reading the Word, and plants them in the heart and spirit.

It is easy to sit down and read a whole chapter of a book in the Bible, or for that matter, a whole Book — but we should ask ourselves, *"how much of what I read is retained in my consciousness?* That approach may be a starting point but better to read a verse or portion of Scripture and meditate on it, allow it to become part of the root network that sustains our life in Christ and makes us fruitful.

In a recent fellowship discussion, which includes someone new in the faith, someone said they found having reference to different translations made it easier to understand the Scriptures. That may be fine for someone who is already established in the faith and in the Word, but there are nuances in language that can change meaning, or the emphasis intended: There are reliable translations[10] among those with subtle changes or omissions, be careful. We may like the way something

---

[10] The New King James (NKJ) the New American Standard (NAS) are reliable translations from the original Hebrew and Greek text. The Amplified Bible provides clarification with parenthetical text.

sounds, comparing one translation to another, but there can be subtle changes to the truth being conveyed. We don't rely on our intellectual ability to comprehend, rather on the ability of the Spirit of God to enlighten our minds with spiritual understanding and wisdom. I would rather encourage anyone to develop intimacy and reliance upon the Spirit of God who dwells within us — He was sent for that very purpose.

> *"In the beginning was the Word and the Word was with God, and the Word was God. He was in the beginning with God. All things were made through Him, and without Him nothing was made that was made. In Him was life, and the life was the light of men. And the light shines in the darkness, and the darkness did not comprehend it...And the Word became flesh and dwelt among us, and we beheld His glory, the glory as of the only begotten of the Father, full of grace and truth"* (John1:5,14).

Christ is the Word. Here is another inviting rabbit trail —

In Christ

As I sit here typing these words, I am **in Christ**! That is the most significant truth revealed in the Word of God.

Previous chapters touch on this same truth from different perspectives, but let's explore more deeply its meaning and application. It is a truth that some of the organized church either misunderstands or simply overlooks in its teaching, which accounts for the sub-culture in Christianity today.

Those words, **"in Christ"** are repeated again and again throughout the New Testament. **I am a new creation, born of the Spirit of God, in Christ**. When we are privileged to come along side someone new in the faith, rather than giving them a list of the "do's and don'ts" of the church — which is like stringing up a tight rope for them to walk on — introduce them to the Holy Spirit and this vital truth — we are "in Christ and His Spirit is in us". The earlier we understand it and acknowledge Christ's right of ownership, the greater the intimacy in our relationship with Him.

It comes back to the matter of connecting the dots. The moment we agreed with God's assessment of us and accepted His provision through Christ to reconcile us to Himself, we were born into the spirit realm of His kingdom - "in Christ": Born of the Spirit of God, a new creation. We are told,

> *"But God, who is rich in mercy, because of His great love with which He loved us, made us alive together with Christ (by grace you have been saved), and raised us up together, and made us sit together in the heavenly places in Christ Jesus ..."* (Ephesians 2:4-6).

That is our place, changing our world view. We become partakers of His divine nature. The challenge to every believer in Christ is giving outward expression of this truth in the way we live — understanding that we can, by the power of the Holy Spirit in us. It becomes a struggle when we allow our emotions or desires of the flesh to control us:

> *"Grace and peace be multiplied to you in the knowledge of God and of Jesus our Lord, as His divine power has given to us all things that pertain to life and godliness, through the knowledge of Him who called us by glory and virtue, by which have been given to us exceedingly great and precious promises, that through these you may be partakers of the divine nature having escaped the corruption that is in the world through lust"* (2 Peter 1:2-4).

The idea that we are no longer our own is not onerous. Jesus said, *"Take my yoke upon you and learn from Me, for I am gentle and lowly in heart, and you will find rest for your souls. For My yoke is easy and My burden is light"* (Matthew 11:29,30). In a sense it is like selling our house but remaining in it as a tenant, having a new landlord who will take better care than we would take ourselves. Since he owns the house we live in, we learn to first consider what pleases him in what we do in and with his house.

God has given us a world full of things to enjoy but as Paul writes, *"All things are lawful for me, but all things are not helpful..."* that is to say they are not profitable or beneficial, they don't contribute to spiritual growth and well-being. He goes on to say, *"All things are lawful for me, but I will not be brought under the power of any"* (1 Corinthians 6:12). Having been delivered from the bondage of sin, Paul says he will not participate in anything that could lead to bondage again.

There was a ten-year period in my life when I allowed other interests to draw me away from the Lord and Christian fellowship. I was encouraged to pursue an opportunity given me to do a television commercial for a new cigarillo. The commercial would be a Viking ship with a Nordic type sailing into New York harbor. I went for test photos and was told I had to be able to inhale the cigarillo smoke for the commercial. Well, I didn't smoke, but my colleagues did - this, before smoke free workspace mandates - so they taught me to inhale.

Let it suffice to say, I didn't get the job: I was twenty-five but photographed like a sixteen-year-old. They were looking for a "weathered" Nordic type - *"...come back in thirty years."* was the answer I got; that and a smoking habit. When the Lord drew me back to Him and Christian fellowship, I found myself bound by the habit - three packs a day. For two years I tried everything to stop smoking because I recognized it as bondage and wanted to be free: Bondage in any form is inconsistent with a life of faith and freedom in Christ. I finally cried out to the Lord for deliverance. To God be the glory - it came from one moment to the next.

If we find ourselves saying, *"I cannot do this or that"*, because I am a Christian, we are responding to a different gospel. There was a movement that swept through Christianity in earlier years calling the saints to "holiness" with the list of things a Christian can and cannot do. The reality of life In Christ is, *"I no longer want to do this or that"*, because I am a new creation in Christ with a new, clean heart and desire to please Him.

In true Christianity our hopes and desires are fixed, not on this world and the things in this world, but on what awaits us; the promises made by God and the inheritance we share with Christ Jesus. A sure sign that we are growing in grace and in the knowledge of our Lord Jesus Christ, is a desire to please Him in all we say and do. *"Does it please Him?"* is the question we ask before acting on an impulse or responding to a desire.

Paul confirms his prayer for the Colossians, *"...may you be filled with the knowledge of His (the Father's) will in all wisdom and spiritual understanding; that you may have a walk worthy of the Lord, (Christ Jesus) **fully pleasing Him**, being fruitful in every good work and increasing in the knowledge of God;* (Colossians 1:9,10 emphasis added). He then proceeds to describe the preeminence of Christ in creation and in redemption. He continues,

> *"As you have therefore received Christ Jesus the Lord, so walk in Him, rooted and built up in Him and established in the faith, as you have been taught, abounding in it with thanksgiving. Beware lest anyone cheat you through philosophy and empty deceit, according to the tradition of men, according to the basic principles of the world, and not according to Christ.*

*For in Him dwells all the fullness of the Godhead bodily and **you are complete in Him**, who is the head of all principality and power"* (Colossians 2:6-10 emphasis added).

There are those words again, *"...you are complete in **Him**...",* meaning there is nothing we can add to what Christ accomplished through the atoning work of the cross. The One in whom we have our being is Christ; and in Him dwells the fullness of the Godhead, bodily. What more can we want, but to please Him?

When the Scriptures say, *"...He shall give you the desires of your heart"* (Psalm 37:4), a phrase commonly quoted out of context, are they saying He will give us whatever we want? No, the first part of the verse sets the tone, *"Delight yourself also in the Lord and He will give you...".* Living in Christ, we learn to align our desires with His, our will with His, pleasing Him and thereby pleasing our Father.

That reminds me of a beloved saint who stood up one Sunday to give the Lord thanks for giving her, *"her heart's desire after many years of asking."* It was a beautiful grand piano - with a five-year payment plan. I should add that knowing her and having been blessed by her life, I know that the real desire of her heart was to know Christ.

Living in Christ, part of His body, are we willing to be spent? Which means placing our energy, our time, our resources, talents and abilities at His disposal, setting aside other interests. That is part of the mind-set being renewed, setting our affection on things above. Yet, as many times as we have heard or read the words, when we come to something we want or something we really want to do, we often forget we are **"in Christ"**. We forget to ask *"does this please Him? Is this what He wants?"*

There are times when we foolishly act as if He is not there or cannot see us, while all the time we are grieving Him and the Holy Spirit. The most egregious rationalization is — *"He knows my heart!"* — for indeed He does, and He sees a love for something else, greater than our love for Him; something we have closed our eyes to. This is the struggle referred to earlier — letting go of the temporal seen things of the world, focusing on the unseen glory prepared by our Father and waiting for us in Christ.

The reality of a Christian is not this world, it is the world to come. Motivated by the Spirit of God in us, we joyfully look forward to the gathering of the saints in Christ, the millennial reign of Christ as Lord and King, and beyond that, a new heaven and a new earth in which only righteousness dwells!

The mighty oak tree is mighty because of its roots. Our root is Christ and the Word of God, which is Christ. Feeding on the Word is the source of our growth and should be a discipline in the life of every Christian and encouraged in anyone new in the faith. There have been and are some wonderful ministers of the Word, who have articulated the truth of God's Word in writings; and thank the Lord for them. But a greater source of wisdom, knowledge and spiritual understanding is available to us in the person of the Holy Spirit who administers the things of Christ, the pure and perfect truth.

How many Christians have a Bible? - how many read their Bible? How many Bibles sit at home, rarely opened?

How many Christians carry a Bible to work, to church, wherever? Today for many, it is the cell phone or other tech device, with the *quick and easy access to the Scriptures **if I want it**;* that is the answer I hear.

There is nothing to be compared with setting time aside knowing we are "in Christ," who desires the intimacy of fellowship with us — holding a Bible, open before the Lord, prayerfully allowing His Spirit to engrave a truth of Scripture on our hearts, our minds and consciousness. The tech device developed by the spirit of the world is programmed to interrupt and distract us. It is not likely to prompt a conversation or introduce an opportunity to witness to someone about the love of God in Christ, that often comes just seeing someone with a Bible.

During thirty-seven years working for the airlines and countless air miles, I can say most of those trips resulted in a conversation with someone about God, about faith or salvation in Christ, prompted by seeing the open Bible.

Even during those desert years of my life when I was not living as I should, I carried and read the Scriptures, and responded to anyone wanting to discuss them.

Perhaps you are asking, "How can that be?" Well, when I finally got to the place where I began to connect the dots, I realized that it is not about me or "us", rather it is the Father working all things through His Son. It is all about Christ Jesus, continually reaching out to man with His message of love and forgiveness, using any and every opportunity and any vessel He chooses to accomplish His purpose.

The seed of God's Word, like the acorn planted and watered, grows. It is not the one who plants or who waters, rather it is God who gives the increase. To Him be the glory.

Chapter Ten

Come and Get It!

Photo: *Me and my nephew Scott and the bell.*

When my family moved to the property on Lake Ontario, the house was not what you might expect to find in a "resort" area. It was an ordinary farmhouse converted into a summer home by the previous owner; nothing special, somewhat austere in appearance. However, there were reminders of a history long since forgotten.

One of them is a mounting block in front of the house that accommodated horse and carriage patrons of what was a summer and winter resort. The house was built in the 1800's. At some point extensions were added on the side and the back of the original farmhouse to facilitate overnight guests at Russell's Island Resort: All but the addition to the living room area had been removed by the time my parents purchased it.

Another reminder was a bell at the back of the house that called everyone to "come and get it" — mealtime. Its peels could be heard all over the island.

In Christianity there is a call to "come and get it" if we are listening with ears to hear — its mealtime, fresh cooked, hot out of the oven. Don't misunderstand, leftovers are good and often taste better because they have been given time to soak up all the flavors — this is true of the Word of God as well and experienced in reading and rereading. But the Spirit of God indwelling the believer in Christ is a cuisine specialist when it comes to preparing a meal: He knows exactly what we need to nourish, strengthen and sustain us.

That new creation "in Christ" needs to be fed in the same way that our natural bodies need daily sustenance. Peter refers to the pure milk of the word – *"...as newborn babes desire the pure milk of the word, that you may grow thereby..."* (1 Peter 2:2); and Paul writing to the saints in Corinth, speaks of wanting to feed them with solid food but he cannot because they are still acting as "mere" men (1 Corinthians 3:1-3).

That is an interesting expression — "acting as mere men". To me it affirms the believer complete in Christ, is more than a mere man; he is all the Father intended

Adam would be and more because of the perfection of Christ, His righteousness. Though we live in this corruptible body, as new creations in Christ and disciples of Christ, we are being transformed by the renewing of our minds, that the outward expression of our lives might be that of Christ and His nature, not of "mere men." *"How is that achieved?"* By feeding on the word of God, relying on the Holy Spirit to make the life "in Christ" a living reality.

We mentioned before our Father's desire for communion and fellowship with His children. We speak to Him in prayer, and He speaks to us through Christ - the written word of God. In my struggles I wrote a song for two voices entitled "Conversation."

Conversation

By David Buisch - 6 November 1981
(For two voices)

Dear father, I agree with You,
that all I say and all I do
apart from Christ is emptiness and loss.
This life of mine is death to me,
but for the cross of Calvary,
where sin and death were crucified,
and I was set free.

My grace and love have made the way,
My truth and light has come to say,
"Come unto Me and I will give you rest.

Just learn of Me, and you will find,
fulfillment, joy and peace of mind.
Take My yoke - it's easy - leave your old
life behind."

Dear Lord, this love I claim for You,
is seldom seen in what I do,
the ways of my old nature, I repeat.
I struggle and I falter as I strive to build my altar,
forgetting that Your sacrifice is full and complete!

I said, "new life in Christ I give,
a life in truth and light to live,
for you, and whosoever will, may come;
and be a free partaker of His life and of His nature, joint
heirs through full adoption - I've made you a Son!"

Dear Father, thank You! …and help be one!

"I have been crucified with Christ; it is no
longer I who live but Christ lives in me; and
the life I now live in the flesh I live by faith
of the Son of God, who loved me and gave
Himself for me" (Galatians 5:20).

This may sound repetitious, but it is a part of Christianity that cannot be over emphasized. There is a significant change that takes place when a person responds to the Gospel and comes to Christ Jesus for salvation — *"Believe on the Lord Jesus Christ, and you will be saved..."*(Acts 16:31). That word *"believe"* is not intellectual acceptance that Christ lived and died. It is the gift of faith energized by the Holy Spirit, believing Jesus is all that He says He is, having done all He says He has done: It is the Holy Spirit's power to draw us and create a sense of need, though we may not fully understand it all at the time.

The transaction that takes place is a new birth by the Spirit of God, **in Christ**, replacing what we were under the power and influence of the spirit of the world, which is antichrist, with a completely new person having or *"partaking of"* the nature of the Son of God: We become a child of God. With our birthright comes a desire for the things of God, to be cultivated by the Holy Spirit through the Word of God. Here is where the significance of John's introduction of Christ Jesus becomes reality for and in us -

> *"In the beginning was the Word, and the Word was with God, and the Word was God. He was in the beginning with God... And the Word became flesh and dwelt among us, and we beheld His glory, the glory of the only begotten of the Father, full of grace and truth"* (John 1:1,14).

So, here we are in Christ, with a new spirit and nature, a clean heart, indwelt by the Spirit of God who creates a desire to know Christ Jesus, or saying it another way, a desire for the Word of God, that we might enjoy communion with Him.

*"But indeed I also count all things **loss for the excellence of the knowledge of Christ Jesus my Lord**, for whom I have suffered the loss of all things and count them as rubbish, that I may gain Christ and be found in Him, not having my own righteousness, which is from the law, but that which is through faith in Christ, the righteousness which is from God by faith; that I may know Him and the power of His resurrection, and the fellowship of His sufferings, being conformed to His death, if by any means, I may attain to the resurrection from the dead. Not that I have already attained, or am already perfected, but I press on that I may lay hold of that for which Christ Jesus has also laid hold of me"* (Philippians 3:8-12 emphasis added).

The earlier we understand the unbreakable connection between Christ and the Word the more we will look forward and make time to feed on the Word of God, because like the apostle Paul, we want to know Christ. Time spent in the Word of God is communion and fellowship with Christ. "But," you say, "I don't feel any particular desire to spend time reading the Bible. Sunday morning in church is enough for me." May I say, if you have indeed accepted Christ Jesus as your Savior and Lord, that desire is there waiting to be energized by the Holy Spirit; He is waiting for you to acknowledge Him and develop intimacy with Him.

We cannot express love of the Lord, in spirit and in truth without the Holy Spirit and a desire to know Christ which is the same as having a desire for the written Word of God. Despite countless efforts to destroy the Scriptures, expunging them from the face of the earth, the Bible remains the best seller of all the books written. The Bible is the revelation of who God is, His attributes and nature, revealed in His Son Christ Jesus. Growing in grace and the knowledge of Christ, feeding on His Word, we grow into the knowledge of who we are in Christ. "Come and get it!"

The world in which we live is under the power and influence of Satan — God in His plan has allowed it for a time. Make no mistake, despite the glitz, glamour and appeal, it is darkness, absent the "light of the world", Jesus!

Some years back when I was working in New York City, a move was made to clean up the image of the Pennsylvania Station; a major undertaking. Penn Station is a transportation hub where bus terminal, commuter trains and subway connections come together. Everything below the ground floor was black, covered with soot. The transformation when the project was completed was amazing — bright and clean. But underlying the silver veneer was the same black soot. That is the way of the world. Though it can give the appearance of light, underneath is darkness.

In contrast, we are new creations in Christ — the darkness of sin has been removed, not covered over. We are in the world, but as the Scriptures say, *"we are not of it"*, neither under its influence nor under its control any longer. Every person who names the name of Jesus as Lord, is here "for such a time as this" representing Him to a world of darkness; that the light of Christ might be seen in and through them.

That is why feeding upon the Word of God is so vital; learning to know Christ and allowing His life to be seen in us. We are a work in progress having been given the Holy Spirit to teach and guide us into all truth — that is, to reveal all that Christ is, His attributes and nature, that they become the outward expression of our lives. "Come and get it"!

Chapter Eleven

Say Your Prayers

"Now I lay me down to sleep, I pray the Lord my soul to keep. If I should die before I wake, I pray the Lord my soul to take. Bless mommy and daddy..."

Thinking back to the time I learned that prayer and eighty years later, it strikes me as a strange prayer to teach a child who has no concept of the significance of the second line – *"if I should die before I wake, I pray the Lord my soul to take."* Yet, those words cut to the core of Christianity.

That prayer itself has an interesting history and many variations on the theme. The innocence of the prayer stands in stark contrast to the reality of the world in which we live: There are many that lay their heads down to sleep with no thought about their soul's destiny. Neither do they question if "tomorrow" will come for them. I say this having had that mind-set for a time, living as though everything would continue as it was.

Prayer for the believer in Christ, is simply talking to our heavenly Father with faith believing that He hears us. In Christianity it is the lifeline of communion with our heavenly Father through Christ Jesus. Jesus, when replying to the disciple's request that He teach them how to pray, said, *"when you pray say:*

> *Our Father in heaven, hallowed be Your name. Your kingdom come, Your will be done on earth as it is in heaven. Give us day by day our daily bread. And forgive us our sins, for we also forgive everyone who is indebted to us. And do not lead us into temptation but deliver us from evil"* (Luke 11:2-4).

It is a beautiful prayer and worthy of repeating, although repetition was not what Jesus had in mind — rather, He was laying out a proper approach to the Father; a structure for prayer or talk with the Father. Prayer is the time a child of God takes to align his thoughts and his will with that of the Father in Christ, regarding every aspect of his life and place in the body of Christ: Looking to the Holy Spirit for help.

The collective prayer of the Church should follow the same example. The Bible reminds us that we don't always know how to pray, underscoring the need to rely upon the Holy Spirit for spiritual wisdom; He prays knowing the mind of Christ. Too often our emotions get in the way — not wanting to see someone suffer we forget that nothing touches a child of God, that God has not permitted and if He has permitted it, He has a purpose in mind. That is why it is so important that while our petition may be specific in nature, we add *"...never-the-less, Your will be done."*

Some will say adding those words is a lack of faith or simply an escape hatch, a way out should God not do what we asked. But in truth it is saying, *"this is what I want but You know better, and I want what You want."* Remember, our Father is working on many fronts through circumstances that touch more lives than the one being tested: So, we pray that His plan and purpose be accomplished — *"...Your kingdom come, Your will be done..."*

Of all the aspects of Christian living, prayer it seems suffers and yet, next to feeding on the Word of God, it is so important. How often does it happen that you purpose in your heart to spend time in prayer — you just get settled down and one thing after the other pops up, distracting or drawing you away from the prayer time you intended; or, as a friend used to complain, "sleep came upon me". Or how many times do we tell someone expressing a need, that we will pray for them - and then forget to pray?

The fact is, the enemy of God and our souls does not want us to pray, it is the battleground of the believer in Christ. There is a common saying that "there is power in prayer", and indeed there is but **the power is in God through prayer**: Praying with faith believing, relying on the Holy Spirit in us who knows the mind of Christ and how we should pray — that is the prayer of "a righteous man that avails much."

I often pondered that thought — *"How can I pray?"* knowing my frailties, *"I am not righteous, so how can my prayer be effective?"*, until I began to connect the dots. Like turning the light on - it's not my righteousness, it is the righteousness of Christ! My part is to bow before Him, align my thoughts and desire with His: *"...Your kingdom come, Your will be done...",* and pray with faith believing as the Spirit within prompts me to pray.

In Christianity, we see the privilege of being a child of God, in prayer. God is all knowing and knows what He is doing because everything to Him is now, free of the constraints of time. *"Does He need our prayer?"* Need, no! Want, yes, as part of His fellowship and communion with us. He enjoins us in prayer, allowing us to be part of what He is doing when we are listening to the Spirit of God in us. In fact, the Scriptures describe that relationship — an interesting rabbit trail.

Is God My Friend?

It is said in the Scriptures that Abraham was a friend of God. There is a natural tendency very much alive in our theology to turn things around. Some of the hymns and contemporary Christian music enjoyed by the saints are good examples of this. Applying human understanding, we divert attention from God or Christ Jesus as the center, to us. In this instance we turn the statement around and say, *"God is our friend".* No, God is the sovereign ruler over all of creation and we are His created image, made His subjects or servants through the atoning work of the cross of Christ. Another aspect of our relationship to Him is that of Father — we are His children: A Father cannot be a friend; he is a father.

Abraham was privileged to be called a friend of God because of his unfaltering faith and obedience. As a friend, God told him what He was about to do. In so doing, He placed Abraham as He did Moses, in a position to involve himself in what God was doing, to intercede, as in the case of Sodom and Gomorrah.

We see the same relationship between Jesus and His disciples in John's Gospel,

> *"This is My commandment, that you love one another as I have loved you. Greater love has no one than this, than to lay down one's life for his friends.*
>
> *You are My friends if you do whatever I command you. No longer do I call you servants, for a servant does not know what his master is doing; but I have called you friends, for all things that I heard from My Father I have made known to you"* (John 15:12-15).

We like to think of Jesus as our friend. It is a comforting thought and brings Him down to our level. But the fact remains that He is our sovereign Lord and Master, not our friend; though He treats us as a friend if we obey His commands. Our relationship to the Father through Christ has many facets - this is but one.

Moses interceded with God on behalf of the children of Israel — and the Scriptures say God repented or had a change of heart. So, what happened? What was going on in the relationship between God and Moses?

Keep in mind that we cannot make God do or persuade Him to do what He does not want to do or is unwilling to do because it does not fit or serve His plan and purpose. God was giving Moses the opportunity to identify with Him, aligning his thoughts and desire with that of the Father — setting his *"affection of things above not on things of the earth."* Did Moses care enough about the children of Israel to intercede for them? - because in truth, God cared about the children of Israel, though they continually offended Him.

In a study of the Palestinian Covenant (Deuteronomy 2729), we see that God entered into that covenant agreement knowing that the children of Israel would not keep their part; telling Moses that they will turn to other gods. But there were two parts to that covenant, one that depended on the response of the children of Israel and a second part of grace which was God's part — *"If we are faithless, He remains faithful; He cannot deny Himself"* (2 Timothy 2:13). We see this same illustration of truth worked out in the intercession of Abraham for Sodom and Gomorrah.

As the body of Christ, we are given endless opportunity to pray, to intercede on behalf of others or for situations that appear hopeless or impossible - but God! When I was born my grandmother Buisch said I looked like a skinned rabbit. According to her account, my body would not accept my mother's milk, cow's milk or any of the formulas they tried; nothing would stay down. This went on for some time creating uncertainty that I would live, so she, my mother and the pastor began interceding for my life in prayer. As I recall being told, it was through a dream that the Lord told my grandmother to give me raw goat's milk. The only baby picture there is of me is a picture of this 'butterball' baby boy - but God!

Intercessory prayer is one form of communication or communion with our Father in Christianity but a vital one.

It is a vital part because it is the battle station of the body of Christ defending against the powers of darkness. It was intercessory prayer Jesus encouraged His disciples to engage in on His behalf, in the garden of Gethsemane.

Photo: My father and mother holding me.

The old saints used to say, *"you take hold of the horns of the altar in prayer, and you don't let go until released by the Spirit of God",* which is an inner sense that you have *"prayed through",* as they used to say: You have been heard and the answer has come or is on the way. That may sound silly, but the warfare that we are engaged in is spiritual, coming against the destructive powers and principalities warring against the Spirit of God and His works.

Prayer also takes the form of simple conversation with Him, thanking and praising Him for who He is, for his faithfulness, love, mercy and grace. It need not be audible - simply from the heart. That kind of prayer reenforces the sense of intimacy we have with our Father, through Christ.

There is nothing to prevent ongoing communion with Him throughout the day in our spirit. That is the relationship Jesus enjoyed with His Father. There is the account of the resurrection of Lazarus, when Jesus says,

"Father, I thank You that You have heard Me. And I know that You always hear Me..." — when all He has said audibly is, if Mary would believe, she would see the glory of God. (John 11:40-42).

Then there is prayer in the form of petitions - requests presented to Him, probably the form most familiar. We are told to make our requests known, even though He knows what we have need of before we ask — to come *"...boldly to the throne of grace, that we may obtain mercy and find grace in time of need."* (Hebrews 4:16).

Regardless of the form or reason we pray - the element of truth and faith must be in it, believing God is who He says He is; we pray **with faith** believing God hears us. How and when He answers is up to Him who has all knowledge and wisdom regarding His plan and purpose. Empty form and repetition of words is not a prayer of faith; I would venture to say it ascends no further than the ceiling. What our Father looks for is prayer from the heart, approaching Him as our Father who loves and cares about His children, simple conversation: He is not impressed by our eloquence or many words and sees through our pretentious piety.

During the years that I coordinated the weekly "prayer meeting" of our church, after a time of collective praise, worship and quietly waiting on the Lord, we would gather in a circle and ask for specific prayer requests before closing. Each one was then asked to present one of the petitions to the Lord in public prayer, one following the other in succession around the circle: This was a way of encouraging participation in public prayer, a simple matter of talking to our Father, for those who were self-conscious about it.

There was one woman who never joined the circle but remained kneeling at the front pew, crying her heart out before the Lord. I assumed she didn't join us because she was not comfortable praying publicly. This went on week after week. Since none of the women approached her, I finally knelt beside her and asked if I could pray with her. I asked if she could share the burden of her heart.

She proceeded to tell me her husband had left her for another woman and how earnestly she had been praying that the Lord would send him home. She didn't understand why the Lord didn't answer her prayer despite her pleading with Him. As I began to pray for her, I attempted to articulate the need by asking the Lord to restore the marriage. Upon hearing those words, she interrupted the prayer telling me,

"Oh no! I want him to come home so I can make him as miserable as he has made me." Need I say more?

When we pray, we look to the Holy Spirit to give us wisdom to know how to pray; that we would have the mind of Christ regarding a situation. I have heard the question asked, *"Is it a lack of faith to present the petition more than once?* In one of the discourses of Jesus, He uses the example of a woman who continues to ask until she gets an answer. I would venture to say the answer to the question depends on the heart of the petitioner.

Where there is complete dependence and trust in our Father to hear and answer our prayer, the number of times we ask would not seem to be important: Jesus, Himself, prayed three times that the bitter cup from which He was about to drink, be removed — adding the third time,

"Nevertheless, not as I will, but as You will" (Matthew 26:39).

So, we ask and then begin to thank Him for what He is doing in response, though there be no outward sign. We live by faith, it is not what we see, but what we know to be true of God, our Father.

Chapter Twelve

The Wart

When WW II ended, we moved to Geneva, New York where my parents bought a house on Seneca Lake (we lived there several years before moving to the house on Lake Ontario). Times were different for children then. The excess in the material things children have today didn't exist, at least not for "poorer" families after the War. Yes, we were poor — not that I was aware of it growing up. I always had clean clothes, although hand-me-downs, food to eat and an imagination that made up for anything I may have felt I lacked.

We were active "all seasons" kids spending most of our free time outdoors. When I was about eight years old that activity became increasingly uncomfortable for me. There was something growing on the calf of my right leg that began to rub against my pantleg. I finally went to my mom and showed her an extremely irritated, good-sized wart. She quietly pulled me into her lap and placed her hand on my leg saying,

"David, we are going to ask Jesus to remove this"; and proceeded to pray. As I sat there to my amazement, the

165

wart literally fell off leaving no trace and the seed of faith was planted in a young heart.

Our mom shared stories about God's intervention in our lives, miraculously healing us when we were little children — a time when both my parents were serving the Lord. I loved to hear them, unaware that that same absolute faith and trust she had, was providing for us and keeping us. There was much going on around me of which I was unaware. I didn't know why our dad didn't live with us, I was just happy to see him on those weekend occasions he did come home: It generally meant we would go to the matinee show at the Regent Theater in Geneva, featuring old sepia-colored western movies. As I approached my teens those visits became more and more infrequent.

Let me preface what you are about to read by saying I love both my parents and saw them both step into eternity "in Christ" - to God be the glory! We have taken trips into the spiritual realm of faith and the grace of God, in previous chapters. We have squarely looked at the incomprehensible wonder of the God of Christianity and the way He works, His ways being past finding out. We simply cannot box Him in. We are going to look at Christianity from the vantage point of being "alive in Christ" with a living faith in the next chapter. So, this is an illustration of all these things working — God's grace.

The apostle Paul suffered an infirmity which when Paul asked that it be removed, God replied, "...*My grace is sufficient for you, for My strength is made perfect in weakness* " (2 Corinthians 12:9).

Well, something had happened in my parent's relationship that created a separation shortly after the end of the War. As I said, I was not aware of anything because my mom never said anything negative about my father, nor did my dad say anything. I learned later in life that my older brother knew what happened, but he too kept it to himself.

It was a severe time of testing for my mom, raising three boys without steady support - but God!

In retrospect, I see the naivety that covered me as providential protection. It was the end of the year 1951. My grandmother Buisch called my mother about a birth notice — a bouncing baby boy born on Christmas day to Mrs. Norman Buisch. It was a few days after that my father approached my mother. His business had failed, and he had neither a place nor means to provide a place for a newborn baby and his mother, *"...would you take them in?"*

According to my mom, her first reaction was "no", but the Lord rebuked her. So, in prayer she asked the Lord to make her willing. You know what? He did! My father had agreed to have no contact with them while they lived with us and so it was that our home was opened, and our lives embraced them. As for me, I was happy to have a baby in the house, totally unaware of the significance of my father's relationship to the event.

They remained with us for a year during which time we came to love them. As God ordained, the mother of the child came to a saving knowledge of Christ while with us, remaining faithful until her death a few years ago.

Oh, the boy? As our Father's providence would have it, my mother and father's relationship was reconciled and they were prepared to adopt him, but his mother decided to take him and move back with her parents.

He was given a new life when his mother married, never knowing about his past. He became an evangelist affiliated with the United Pentecostal Church, and later a pastor. When he was twenty-four years old however, having accidentally learned who his paternal father was, he searched until he found us. A joyful reunion and finally the answer to the question he always had — *" why don't I look like my brothers?"*

He was tall, blond and fair-skinned, whereas his brothers were shorter in stature with dark hair and darker complexion.

Chapter Thirteen

Alive or Dead?

It was one of those perfect summer days, the sun high in a cloudless sky. I heard the bell, so knew it was lunchtime and was making my way home from adventures in the back forty. Barefoot from the time school ended, the soles of my feet were like leather. As I walked along the dirt road that took you back to Blind Creek, I saw movement and heard noise in the tall grass on the side of the road. As I continued to walk, I realized something was in the grass keeping pace alongside me. The grass was thick so I couldn't see what it was but after a quick calculation I figured I could intercept it if I stepped in at the right moment.

Perfect timing — and I am standing there holding a woodchuck by the scruff of the neck. Initially it squirmed, but like a cat that becomes limp when you pick it up by the scruff of the neck, the woodchuck became limp. It was not long before I realized the poor thing had fainted. As I approached the house, I laid the woodchuck which I assumed was still breathing, on the picnic table thinking it would revive and be on its way. My dad came in a short time later -

"What's that dead woodchuck doing out there on the picnic table?"

Alive or dead? I meant no harm to the woodchuck, and it looked alive when I left it on the picnic table - but it was dead. The Christian in Christianity is said to be alive "in Christ". We were dead in trespasses and sin but have been made alive in Christ by the redeeming love of God, and the atoning work of the cross of Christ Jesus. *What is it - to be alive in Christ?*

First and foremost is to realize that we have eternal life, that though we may die in this physical realm, our bodies being corruptible, yet we live hidden with Christ in God. That is, life forever, outside of time, a dimension we have difficulty grasping.

Do the people around us know that we are Christians? — that is the starting point of this field trip. I spent my entire working years, working in an office environment. Perhaps because I would ask or show interest, many of my colleagues shared their lives - family and interests, and in some instances, faith. Some considered their faith too personal to share or talk about. I shared my life in the same manner with them including my faith.

The same was true during my four-year stint in the Navy. It was divided between some shore duty and duty aboard ship. I thoroughly enjoyed the time on the ship and particularly time spent at sea. Looking back, I see our Father's provision for me.

My rating was Personnel man, and I was initially assigned to the personnel office where five of us worked.

We were told that a new navigator had been assigned to the ship and would be looking for a yeoman to work with him.

As it happened, one morning the top of the Dutch door to the office flew open and in a thundering voice the new Navigator, a Lieutenant Commander, introduced himself. His voice alone was so intimidating I turned my back and tried to look as busy as I could. Over the next few days, he would appear unexpectedly, saying nothing. My workstation was directly opposite the door, so each time, my back to the door, I would keep my head down hoping he didn't notice me.

Then one morning that door flew open and all I heard in that thundering voice was, *"I want you!"*. No one said a word, so I slowly turned in my chair to see him standing there pointing at me. With that gesture, I became yeoman to the Navigator and Captain's speaker, with an office one deck below the flying bridge. It was a comfortable working space, small but room enough for a typing desk and a visitor's chair. I even had music (a record player) and

Photo: *USS Vulcan*

pictures on the wall that gave me a good indication of the list of the ship in rough seas.

I could not have asked for better duty or a more pleasant man with whom to work. One of my duties was transcribing the ship's log which detailed the reports of the officer's watch covering the twenty-four-hour day. There was a deadline for submitting the typed log with officers' signatures below their entry. It had to be perfect — no typos, and no erasures or type-over corrections, so quiet concentration was important: Thank the Lord for His enabling. Getting the officers to sign the log was something else - like chasing rabbits, but that is not the point of sharing this.

Because it was a quiet, out of the way space, different ones of my shipmates would drop in to talk: All knew where it was because the Navigator authorized liberty passes which I issued. The conversations would be during after duty hours, and for the most part I just listened as they unloaded whatever was on their mind, only offering advice or an opinion if asked.

There was one young seaman who came more and more frequently. We had lengthy conversations touching on the more significant issues of life and faith. He had trouble at home - all was not well with his girlfriend.

It was apparent he was dealing with some unsettled issues and the ship was scheduled to leave Norfolk for the Caribbean and training maneuvers at sea. We would be gone for two or three months which meant no shore leave in the States. My attempts at encouragement failed to reach him.

It was the weekend before our departure and I was preparing for shore leave with some buddies, when he popped his head in the door of the office —

"Got a minute? I need to talk."

I looked at my watch and told him I didn't have time, "How about tomorrow? I've got a liberty pass and just about to leave - why don't you come with us?"

There was no response, he simply walked away and that was the last time I talked to him.

It was Monday morning that I heard he was AWOL. He had a weekend pass and went home. Most of the day Monday was spent trying to find out what happened — sadly and tragically, he shot himself because his girlfriend broke up with him.

It took some time to get beyond the initial shock and lingering sense of guilt for having failed him: *Why didn't I take the time to talk? Would it have made a difference?*

Did I discuss my faith with him? Yes, but looking back I saw that being "alive in Christ" would have produced a living faith, one that would have regarded his well-being more important than the shore leave I had planned. When we talked about God and faith, being alive in Christ, I would have inquired to know if his faith was indeed in Christ Jesus and Him alone.

We are exploring true Christianity: There is a sensitivity energized by the Spirit of God in us, to the things going on around us when we are alive in Christ. We are approachable and available to be spent, looking for and seeing opportunities to invest in the kingdom of God — a living faith because we are alive in Christ.

In this account of the young seaman, I was one who openly confessed my faith in Christ Jesus — but failed to live it when given the opportunity. I don't know why it takes so long for some of us to connect the dots - connecting "being alive in Christ" with "a living faith". But then, "you can't get there until you get there!" and our Father is faithful, having begun a good work in us, to complete it.

Do you remember singing, *"This little light of mine, I'm going to let it shine, this little light of mine, I'm going to let it shine, let it shine, let it shine, all the time."*? It is a delightful children's song like, *"I'll be a sunbeam for Jesus"*. But when do those words become reality? Presumably when we come to Christ Jesus and experience the love, mercy and grace of God, through the atoning work of the cross.

> *"You are the light of the world. A city that is set on a hill cannot be hidden. Nor do they light a lamp and put it under a basket, but on a lampstand, and it gives light to all who are in the house. Let your light so shine before men that they may see your good works and glorify you Father in heaven"* (Matthew 5:14-16).

If we find our faith is too personal to share, we are not living in truth, nor are we appropriating all that our Father has provided, that we might be conformed to the image of His Son. **We are the body of Christ** living in a world of darkness. What did Jesus mean when He said, *"this is My* *body which is broken for you"?* His physical body was not broken; beaten beyond recognition, yes - tortured by crucifixion, yes but not broken. Then breaking the bread, He passed it to each disciple, each breaking off a piece and eating it. To me, it symbolized the distribution of Himself among His disciples, His Church; His nature, love and humility, each piece a part of one heavenly bread.

Sadly, there is much activity that falls under the name "Christianity", which would more accurately be called religion, according to the world's definition. Some of the teaching being promoted in the organized church follows a human philosophy. There are portions of Scripture that don't fit the theology, so they are simply ignored. The result, measured against the truth of the Word of God, is a dead religion, absent the power of the Holy Spirit, the gifts of the Holy Spirit, the fruit of the Holy Spirit and reliance upon Him in all that we say and do — "in the name of Jesus". The realization of this sub-culture in Christianity inspired a song -

Wake Up My Child

by David Buisch - 21 January 1982

I've made a way for you - wake up My
child! and follow Me!
All you have to do, is come, believe and be!
Wake up My child, abide in me,
by faith you live in victory.
I've made a way for you - wake up My child
and live!

You're branches of the Vine – wake up
My child, I've work to do!
Your life's not yours, it's Mine, for I
have chosen you.
Wake up My child, My vessel clean,
our Father's love is to be seen.
You're branches of the Vine - wake up My
child and live!

I said, "I'll soon return."
Wake up My child, you've slept too long!
Awake your heart would burn with love's
triumphant song
Wake up My child and hear the cry,
as those around in darkness die.
I said, "I'll soon return." Wake up My child
and live!

One of the great problems in the church both collectively and individually is denial or hiding from the truth. We become dogmatic, that is, unwilling to consider or concede that we may be wrong. Is our faith so fragile that we close our mind to truth for fear of losing it? We are given this wonderful revelation of truth but refuse to let it speak for itself, because when we do, we find our theology may be lacking. The tendency is to fix our mind on what we have accepted as the final interpretation or understanding of a portion of Scripture, and then use or manipulate the Word to make it fit that understanding.

In contrast, revelation by the Spirit of God in us, opens our understanding as we grow in grace and in the knowledge of Christ. The result is increased knowledge and spiritual understanding as more light is received through meditation and revelation of the Holy Spirit. That's why Paul, talking about pressing toward *"...the goal for the prize of the upward call of God in Christ Jesus."* writes,

> *"Therefore, let us, as many as are mature, have this mind, and if in anything you think otherwise, God will reveal even this to you. Nevertheless, to the degree that we have already attained let us walk by the same rule, let us be of the same mind"* (Philippians 3:15,16).

To my understanding, in Christianity there is none who has attained complete knowledge and spiritual understanding of the Word of God, because we are all a work in progress this side of glory. That is not to say that as we mature, we have not arrived at a point concerning a certain truth that we absolutely know and understand — we do: But it is supported by the whole counsel of God.

Part of this aspect of being alive in Christ, is the desire for fellowship in the Word. If we allow Him, the Holy Spirit gives us the ability to discuss and agree to disagree when one or the other cannot be persuaded along a particular line of reasoning: We leave the enlightenment to the Holy Spirit, the Spirit of truth.

When we come to the Word with a desire to know, using a familiar portion of Scripture as an example, we often find there is a greater depth of spiritual understanding or another dimension to what we thought we understood. That is the reason I have hesitated to write a book. There can be nothing more disheartening to an author than to find after publication, that he or she has fallen short of the truth for lack of "knowing" or for lack of "spiritual understanding". Thankfully, our Father's interest in the growth and well-being of all His children covers our frailties: But even more reason to encourage and underscore the importance of fellowship in the Word— *"...till we all come to the unity of the faith and the knowledge of the Son of God, to a perfect man, to the measure of the stature of the fullness of Christ"* (Ephesians 4:13). Alive in Christ!

Chapter Fourteen

Clocks and Calendars

Our society is bound to time, schedules and calendars - clocks are everywhere. The history of calendars is interesting; using access to the Internet and a web site like Wikipedia, one can see how far back in the recorded history of man's existence, calendars were part of a society. Our focus as adherents of the Christian faith, Christianity, is the Scriptures or the Bible, which in a sense places us in two different worlds: One being that of the Hebrew calendar and the other being the Gregorian Calendar universally used by the nations of the world in secular matters today — an interesting field trip.

Most of us use a calendar to keep track of appointments, meetings, events and activities relating to business, home, children's activities and church, whatever. A frustration when working as a Human Resource, Personnel manager, was the call from the executive over me, detailing his calendar for the year involving my participation: It was like seeing my life being spent before I got out of the starting gate.

God too, has a calendar, however nonspecific as relating to time because He is outside of time. As mentioned before, God can be so specific as to name the month, the day and the hour of certain events in the recorded relationship with His people, yet totally ignore detail in other instances. He refers to specific years — as in *"Josiah was eight years old when he became king, and he reigned thirty-one years in Jerusalem"* (2 Kings 22:1) and refers to ages and tells what is going to happen, but not when. Why?

"The just shall live by faith.", that's why. Through the Word of God, He tells us what He wants us to know or what we need to know to understand what He is doing: The bottom line is, we either trust Him or we don't! That said, there is the natural tendency to attempt creating a calendar from what we are given to know, albeit incomplete information. Consider for a moment that the early church expected that Christ would return at any time and lived accordingly. Here we are, nearly two thousand years later still waiting — but are we expecting His return and are we living as though Christ could come for the Church at any time?

Some men of faith, esteemed by the church, lost their luster because they falsely declared the day of Christ's return; in some cases, more than once when the first failed to happen. Some have used natural phenomenon in failed attempts to predict future events talked about in the Bible. Jesus, talking to His disciples foretells the destruction of the temple in Jerusalem, prompting the questions, *"Tell us, when will these things be? And what will be the sign of Your coming, and of the end of the age?"* In Matthew's account of that discussion (Matthew 24), Jesus referring to the His second coming and the end of the age says, *"of that day and hour no one knows; no not even the angels in heaven, but My Father only."*(Matthew 24:36) — and here's a rabbit trail:

Christ's Reappearance

The Bible talks about two separate appearances of Jesus yet to come in God's calendar. The first will be in the clouds — when He comes to gather the saints, His Church, also referred to as His Bride, to be with Him. He will not set foot on the earth, but will appear in the clouds –

> *"For the Lord Himself will descend from heaven with a shout, with the voice of an archangel and with the trumpet of God. And the dead in Christ will rise first. Then we who are alive and remain shall be caught up together with them in the clouds to meet the Lord in the air. And thus, we shall always be with the Lord"* (1 Thessalonians 4:16,17).

This is the event in God's calendar that is referred to as the "rapture" of the Church of Jesus Christ, although the word "rapture" does not appear in Scripture. It is the removal of the Church before Christ literally returns to earth.

The second appearance is when He returns **to earth**, that is, literally sets foot on the earth at the end of the great tribulation period. He returns to destroy the godless, the enemies of God, bind Satan and *"cast him into the bottomless pit, and shut him up, and set a seal on him, so that he should deceive the nations no more till the thousand years were finished"* (Revelation 20:3). That event is referred to as the Second Coming of the Lord. What follows is His millennial reign, having established His throne in Jerusalem where He rules and reigns over the nations for a thousand years.

There are different schools of thought concerning these future events and what happens during that seven-year period in which the great tribulation takes place. Our Father has seen fit to keep the details hidden, consequently the position of the Church in relation to the unfolding of events is not clear.

There are those that believe the Church of Jesus Christ will go through the great tribulation, during which the wrath of God is unleashed on the world (Revelations). Another belief is that the Church will be removed before the great tribulation, because as children of God we are saved from His wrath — we are not children of wrath. The third belief is that the world is currently living in the millennial reign of Christ.

But here is something to think about. We cannot know the day or hour or even the exact year of His coming, but we are encouraged to watch and observe the signs of the times. An overview of the conditions of the world right now would seem to meet all the criteria described in Scripture relating to the mystery of the assembling of the saints and the second coming of the Lord, increased lawlessness, violence and apostasy of the church.

There is no exact record of the birth of Jesus, day, month or year, therefore no exact record of the year of His death and resurrection. A commonly accepted reconstruct based on other historical writings and information places His birth as early as 6 BC or around the year 4 BC; correspondingly, His death and resurrection based on His age, would be somewhere between AD 27 and AD 29.

We are fast approaching the end of the two thousand-years since the death and resurrection of Christ based on what has been reconstructed regarding the life of Jesus. The Scriptures say,

> *"But, beloved, do not forget this one thing, that with the Lord one day is as a thousand years, and a thousand years as one day"* (2 Peter 3:8).

Assuming there is significance in the above Biblical text, other than understanding that God is outside of time and time constraints, we would be wise to consider that we are about to come to the end of day two in time, (two thousand years), since the resurrection of Jesus and His ascension. There is a correlating reference to the future of the Jews, found in the Old Testament book of Hosea:

> *"Come, and let us return to the Lord:*
> *For he has torn, but He will heal us:*
> *He has stricken, but He will bind us up.*
> *After two days He will revive us:*
> *On the third day He will raise us up,*

That we may live in His sight" (Hosea 6:1,2).

It will soon be two thousand years since the Jews rejected their Messiah, Christ the Lord.

There is a general understanding of Scripture that the Church Age ends when the Church of Jesus Christ is gathered to Him, or removed from earth, commonly referred to as the Rapture. This takes place sometime in the last seven years before Christ literally steps foot on earth the second time: The second coming of the Lord. I believe what follows in the last three and a half years, the period of the Great Tribulation, is a period of great awakening among both Jews and Gentiles, focusing on the Jewish people - *"...after two days He will revive us..."*, and ending the Age of the Gentiles.

According to the Book of the Revelation of Jesus Christ to the churches, the last three and a half years, culminate in the glorious victory of Christ over the enemies of God and His Christ and those who have moved against Israel. Christ will then establish His kingdom in Israel and His throne in Jerusalem; the beginning of His millennial reign - *"...on the third day He will raise us up..."*; restoring the glory of Israel and Jerusalem as promised.

If God's calendar in time, runs in periods of one thousand years, the events leading up to the seven years prophesied by Daniel are upon us, as is the rapture of the Church — assuming we believe we are saved from the wrath of God to come on all unrighteousness. In which case these events are forerunners or preludes to the revelation of the antichrist, the great tribulation and the second coming of the Lord. Day three begins the millennial reign of Christ: The number three represents a fullness of time. What follows day three (three thousand years) according to the Bible, is the final triumph and glorious victory of Christ over all the enemies of God, destroying Satan and death. Then the end of this earth as we know it gives way to new heavens, the new earth and the new Jerusalem descending from above; gives me goosebumps.

It is difficult to ignore the parallel between the glorious resurrection of Jesus three days after His death and His final glorious victory, three days (three thousand years) after His resurrection. All this to say, though we are not given to know the day, hour or for that matter the year, now is not the time for the believer in Christ Jesus to slack off. Rather, now is the time to press in and press on, place our lives on the line to be spent in the advancement of the kingdom of God - to God be the glory!

Oh, that He would find us grounded and rooted in His Word, strengthened by the Spirit of God in us to stand against the persecution intended by the spirit of antichrist to weaken and destroy those who are "in Christ". That spirit is already working in the world against Christianity. That He would find us ready, watching and expecting to hear a shout and the sound of a trumpet — when we shall rise to meet Him in the air!

Many years ago, a song was inspired while meditating on the Word and contemplating the return of Jesus in the clouds to gather the saints -

My Lord is Coming Soon

By David Buisch - 3 January 2000

A day like any other as the morning sun appears.
The world, about its business
midst anxiety and fears
is unaware that this is not an ordinary day;
and something deep inside makes
me want to shout and say -
He's coming, He's coming, morning, night or noon!
He's coming Hallelujah! My Lord is coming soon!

I feel my heart beat faster
as I search the eastern sky,
for something's different in the air,
although I don't know why.
No sound of birds, a silence like
the lull before the storm,
awaiting introduction
as the clouds begin to form -

He's coming, He's coming, morning night or noon!
He's coming, Hallelujah! My Lord is coming soon!

The Heavenly host surrounds the throne
awaiting God's command,
the Father turns to Jesus
sitting there at His right hand.
A holy hush has fallen;
the Father's will be done -
No sound is heard until the words are spoken,

"Now, My Son!"

Hear the trumpet! Can you see Him?
Clouds of glory in the sky!
We are caught up, Hallelujah!
In the twinkling of an eye!

What we can know of God's calendar is this –

- a move against Israel, in which God intervenes to protect Israel, (Ezekiel 38);

- a peace accord with Israel which begins the seventh- year period referred to in Daniel, (Daniel 9);

- Israel will rebuild the temple in Jerusalem somewhere in this time frame.

- The peace accord will be broken after three and a half years, which begins the great tribulation period, *(somewhere in this seven-year period, the Church of Jesus Christ will be raptured, taken out of the world and the antichrist will be revealed)*; followed by the second coming of the Lord; the battle of Armageddon and temporary confinement of Satan (Revelation 19,20);

- Christ's millennial reign over all the nations from Jerusalem (Revelation 20);

- followed by the last and final battle where all the enemies of God are destroyed, Satan and death are cast into the lake of fire (Revelation 20);
- followed by the resurrection of the dead and great White Throne judgement (Revelation 20);
- lastly the new heavens and earth, and new Jerusalem descending, after the heavens and earth we now know are dissolved (Revelation 21).

That's some calendar as I understand it from the Scriptures! But let me be quick to point out that my understanding is limited. The point is, we are privileged to be given a peek into what our Father is doing, through the prophets and the Revelation of Jesus Christ to the churches.

One significant observation seen in His calendar is the single-minded purpose of God, keeping His promises, His Word. His promises to Abraham, His covenant with His chosen people the Jews; His Word regarding Israel and Jerusalem, and the Church of Jesus Christ; these are the focus of God throughout the Scriptures. As mentioned at the outset of this excursion, Israel and Jerusalem are the only pieces of real estate on which God has placed His name and His seal. Everything God has said regarding the restoration and glory of Israel and Jerusalem, will happen.

The other more significant observation is the exaltation and glorification of His Son Jesus, the Christ. Everything is centered in Him and on Him until all the enemies of God and His Christ are destroyed. It is then that Christ Jesus gives everything back to the Father, submitting to His eternal power and rule.

Chapter Fifteen

Ears to Hear

As a child I was told I looked just like my grandfather Buisch. Now I will admit to being a strange child, overly sensitive and naive with strange notions. As an example, I thought if you broke an arm, it fell off. I was a teenager and believed that if you kissed a girl you had to marry her: Imagine the shock when a classmate of mine kissed me — we were playing a game, hiding under some bushes when she upped and kissed me — on the mouth! I think I solved the dilemma by rationalizing - she kissed me; I didn't kiss her.

Photo: *My Grandfather Buisch*

Getting back to my grandfather, he was a somewhat austere looking man with a disposition to match, although I only experienced a gentler side seldom seen. Between the ages of two and four, I spent a lot of time with my grandparents due to my mother's health. I have memories of being held on his lap, riding for hours while he plowed the field. Somewhere in that time the comment was made about looking like him and it scared me.

My grandfather was a big man, tall, but the thing that struck me as a child was his ears; to me they were very big. So, I grew up with the fear that I would have big ears like his. Thank the Lord, I forgot about it and only thought of it in connection with this field trip.

The size of our ears has little to do with our ability to hear. In the natural world, there are any number of things that can affect our hearing ability. However, In the spiritual world our ability to hear is not the issue, rather a matter of the heart and our wanting to hear — what I would call "selective hearing."

It reminds me of business trip encounter. I was seated in First Class (a courtesy), where it is easier to converse without bothering anyone else. The man sitting next to me engaged me in conversation. As it happened, we were just passing over Lake Ontario, and I commented that it was where my father lived. He began to ask me questions about my father, and as I talked about him, he said, *"From the way you talk, you must have had a wonderful relationship with your father,* to which I replied, *"No, in fact I had little or no relationship with him until I was in my thirties."*

Upon hearing that, he expressed sorrow over his own failed relationship with his children, *"I've been too busy. No time for them when they were young and impressionable."*

From what he said, all attempts to bond with them now, were rebuffed. So, I began to tell him how the Lord through the Scriptures, healed my relationship with my father, encouraging him that it is never too late and that all things are possible with God. I shared my experience and the way the Lord used the 139th Psalm to show me His sovereign grace working in my life before my parts were formed: That revelation inspired a letter I wrote to my dad telling him I loved him and that I thanked God, he was my father.

He listened intently wanting to know what happened, how my dad reacted. That gave me the opportunity to share what the Lord did in my father's heart. As we talked, I found myself telling him about an incident that happened during a business trip to Anchorage, Alaska. I don't recall the reason I was there but recall the incident as if it happened yesterday. It speaks to the truth that with God all things are possible:

Whatever the business was, I was there for five business days, so I looked for and found a church that had a Wednesday evening service which I attended. At the close of the service, I went to the altar to pray. Part of my prayer was, *"Father, I have to be here, so please let it not be wasted time."*

Anchorage was not the city it is today. Roads were still being paved and as I would learn, street lighting was limited. The church was located some distance from the center of town, so it was a good walk from my hotel. It was still daylight when I arrived at the church, but the sun had set by the time I started back to the hotel. Making my way in darkness, I heard a voice behind me saying, *"Excuse me—excuse me!"*

I turned but didn't immediately see anyone but heard the voice again, *"Excuse me—excuse me Sir!"* and a man appeared walking his bicycle.

He continued, *"Are you by any chance, a Christian?"*

I replied yes, and before I could say anything else he said, *"Would you have time—I need to talk to someone."*

We walked a short distance and found a bench set back from the road with a dim light shining over it - it was apparently a play field. We sat down and crying, he began to pour out his heart: His wife left him, he had lost his business, and lost what little faith he had, questioning the love of God.

He didn't offer any detail as to how or why the events shattering his life happened, and I didn't probe, but as I began trying to comfort him, I found myself saying, *"God loves you and knows right where you are—think for a moment. How did you happen to stop me? — and in the dark."*

He was quiet for a moment, *"I don't know, in fact something threw me over the handlebar of my bike. I don't know what happened, but If that had not happened, I would have missed you"*; with that he pointed to his torn pant leg and bloody knee.

"What you don't know", I said, *"is, I don't live here, I am from New York, and I am only here for five days; and you think God doesn't love you. I would say He loves you very much."*

We talked for a time, and I shared some Scripture with him, thankful for the dim light. Then we prayed together, asking the Lord to restore his faith, marriage and his business.

That Christmas I received a card from him saying he had moved to Arizona. God restored his marriage; he had a thriving business, and they found a local church and were serving the Lord - together.

I could see in the face of my travel companion, that he was moved. We continued to talk but as the conversation moved closer to the issue of his own relationship to Christ Jesus, he said abruptly, *"Stop, I don't want to hear any more.",* and repositioned himself in his seat, remaining silent for the rest of the trip. The Spirit of God was speaking to him, but he didn't want to hear anymore.

As I pondered that, it occurred to me that he somehow knew that if he heard more, he would be responsible for what he heard and for his reaction or response. What he didn't know, was our meeting was not a coincidence and somewhere down the road there would be another intercept.

The Spirit of God is continually speaking to us through the Word of God, through circumstances and the situations we face in life, if we will listen:

"Therefore, my beloved brethren let every man **be swift to hear, slow to speak,** *slow to wrath: For the wrath of man does not produce the righteousness of God"* (James 1:19 emphasis added).

We are inclined to do just the opposite, quick to speak and slow to listen.

I can still hear myself saying under my breath, *"I hear you, but I'm not listening.",* when my dear mom, concerned for my soul, would try to tell me I was in danger. We do that so often to the Spirit of the Lord, perhaps not saying it but by our attitude and action. When we allow our emotions to control our actions or reactions, our responses to situations, we are not listening. When we have determined to do something regardless of roadblocks God places in our path, we are not listening. When we sit through a teaching or a sermon and gleaned nothing for ourselves but think only that so-in-so should have been there to hear it, we are not listening. We have ears to hear, and the ability to hear the Spirit of God in us, if we will listen: His cautionary words touch every area of our lives. When the time comes to gather the saints, may we be listening, found "in Christ" and where He is. That reminds me of a chorus the Lord gave me years ago:

I'm Taken Up with Jesus

By David Buisch - 14 September 1985

I'm taken up with Jesus He's the
lover of my soul.
Since Jesus took me up with Him His life
has made me whole!
There's nothing here to hold me,
For I am heaven bound -
So don't be sad, for I am glad,

So very, very, very glad to know Him
and where He is, be found!

The warning of God's coming judgement in the parable of the tares, ends with the words, *"He who has ears to hear, let him hear"* (Matthew 13:43). The message given to each of the churches in the Revelation of Jesus, closes with these words: *"He who has an ear, let him hear what the Spirit says to the churches."* The messages reveal what Christ sees: He sounds an alarm, but also offers encouragement to the one who overcomes. Are we listening?

The organized church is in trouble and the Church of Jesus Christ is facing persecution — it is already happening. *"Watch and pray!"*. May I encourage you to give time to prayer, interceding for believers across the globe, that each one be strengthened in the inner man, taking *"...up the whole armor of God, that you (they) may be able to withstand in the evil day, and having done all, to stand"* (Ephesians 6:13 emphasis added).

Chapter Sixteen

Alle, Alle, Auch Sind Frei

How many times as a kid, did I hear those words on a warm summer night after dark. I don't think any of us playing hide and seek or kick the can, had any idea what we were saying. The German expression sounded like "oly, oly, oxen free" to us, but its meaning was the same; and having nothing to do with oxen it became *"oly, oly, home free"* for many — someone made it home, it is safe, you can come out now. I don't remember all the rules of those games but remember the exhilaration of trying to reach home or kick the can without being caught, particularly when played after dark.

In the spiritual realm and those things pertaining to the kingdom of God, there is one who has made it "home" for us: Christ Jesus, the Son of Man, who endured the cross having put sin out of the way through the atonement. Restored to His rightful place in all His glory through His glorious resurrection from the dead, He calls to all who have an ear to hear.

This is our last field trip. The adherents of Christianity, that is, true believers in Jesus Christ and Him alone, are fast approaching that time when the equivalent of the German expression *"all, all, come in"*, will be heard. It will happen quickly and without warning - Christ Jesus will appear in all His glory in the clouds with the sound of a trumpet and a shout, to gather the saints to Himself.

Connecting the dots in the meantime, that is, the spiritual understanding given us by the Spirit of God in us, we know that we are here for such a time as this. In the opening prayer of the 117th Congress, our representatives just publicly distanced themselves from the faith and the belief of our nation's founding fathers in the **one true God**. For the first time in our nation's history the prayer was offered up in the names of all the gods of all religious beliefs.

Foreboding clouds have been forming on the horizon for some time. Christians in many parts of the world are already the target of persecution, violence and death. At the same time, there is a mighty move of God's Spirit across the globe drawing men and women to faith in Christ Jesus. Until now, we have enjoyed the freedom of "religious expression" guaranteed by our Constitution, but — brace yourself!

We are encouraged through the Scriptures to *"...put on the whole armor of God."* which equips us for defensive spiritual warfare, individually and collectively. The use of the word "warfare" alarms some who would read it as though Christianity is a violent faith and ideology. However, the opposite is true. The very foundation of Christianity rests on the fact that *"God so **loved** the world that He gave..."*

The gospel message is by way of invitation, not oppression: Each person is free to choose. It is Satan, the prince and power of the air, the ruler of darkness, who has declared war, directing all his energy and activity against God, His works and His people: He has but one desire and that is to destroy them. He cannot undue the work of the cross of Christ Jesus — that is a finished, complete work, though he (Satan) thought the death of Jesus, would thwart God's plan.

There is an aggressive element in the warfare in which the believer in Christ finds himself. It is not with material weapons, rather with prayer — intercessory prayer energized by the Holy Spirit: *"For the weapons of our warfare are not carnal but mighty in God for pulling down strongholds, casting down arguments and every high thing that exalts itself against the knowledge of God..."*

Now, the tendency is to stop there, but there is more, *"...bringing every thought into captivity to the obedience of Christ and being ready to punish all disobedience when your obedience is fulfilled"* (2 Corinthians 10:46).

That is our warfare individually and collectively; intercessory prayer on behalf of the Church - the believers in Christ. That each one naming the name of Christ Jesus, would bring *"...every thought into captivity to the obedience of Christ, and being ready to punish all disobedience when your obedience is fulfilled."*

During this recent presidential election cycle (2020) a great deal of time and energy has been spent praying for our nation. I have no doubt every Christian is grieved seeing what has been happening in our country - the arrogance in our attitude toward God. I wish it were otherwise. Invoking God's word to the children of Israel found in 2 Chronicles is misplaced faith: Israel was the land given by God to His chosen people. It is the only land and nation on which He has placed His name and seal.

Would it not be wonderful, if in the natural world we could turn the clock back eighty years to a time when there was wide public consciousness of God? It was a time when there was still a national innocence, and a moral standard: World War II ended that. Those that faced and returned from the horrors of war and those that lived through the years of struggle and deprivation, sought peace, security and rest: Enjoyment of the natural comforts of life.

A subtle change began to take place. The nation continued to use the words "In God We Trust" and "God Bless America", but under the subtle influence of the spirit of antichrist the dependence upon God has slowly, over time warped into dependence on our own strength and ability as a nation, to rebuild and maintain freedom. We as believers in Christ are citizens of heaven. Our sights should be set on the kingdom of God. The truth is, the way of the world is never the way of repentance, turning around and going back. Nothing will be the same from this day forward, but we "in Christ" are encouraged to *"Stand in the ways and see, and ask for the old paths, where the good way is, and walk in it; then you will find rest for your souls"* (Jeremiah 6:16).

So, as Christians, we keep our minds focused on what God is doing to accomplish His will and purpose — *"...Your kingdom come, Your will be done..."*. God shows us throughout the Bible, that He uses nations and leaders of nations to accomplish His purpose. He has abundantly blessed our nation since its foundation, and used it to bless other people, nations throughout the world. It is all part of His plan, just as He used Pharaoh and King Cyrus in Old Testament times. He also judges nations because He must if He is true to Himself and His righteousness: God does not save nations apart from Israel, for His name's sake; He saves people.

Christianity is all about seeing God for who He is; seeing His love expressed through the sacrifice of His Son Jesus. It is about relationship, both with God the Father through Christ, and with Christ through the work of the Holy Spirit. It is seeing and understanding our place in Christ; our place in the body of Christ and the need to be conformed to His image if we are to represent Him to the world around us, as He is.

The world looks at Christianity and sees the imperfection of the organized church. It refuses to acknowledge the good will, the good works and contribution to society made over centuries by Christianity:

> "For we are His workmanship created in Christ Jesus for good works, which God prepared beforehand that we should walk in them" (Ephesians 2:10).

Christianity is labeled a threat to social order today. Christians are being told in so many words, they must abandon strict adherence to the Word of God, to conform to a new world order of inclusiveness.

Fortunately, we can look with eyes of faith beyond this physical realm and see what our Father sees. He sees the Church, the Bride of Christ, without spot or wrinkle. He sees perfection, because Christ Jesus is perfect and we who believe in Him and Him alone, are in Him, covered by His righteousness. But we are here now, for such a time as this. We should not close our eyes to our collective failure as the church and body of Christ, if we are to know how to pray for the church.

Defeat of Victory

We are not playing a childhood game of hide and seek in Christianity; hiding until we can get home. The Church of Jesus Christ is a glorious, victorious Church — because Christ Jesus is glorious and victorious. That is a truth nothing can change.

But the Word of God tells us that a time is coming when men and women will turn away from the truth. The apostle Paul warns young Timothy –

> *"For the time will come when they will not endure sound doctrine, but according to their own desires because they have itching ears, they will heap up teachers; and they will turn their ears away from the truth, and be turned aside to fables"* (2 Timothy 4:3,4).

There is a great danger in hiding from truth, both individually and collectively: That time is here, happening all around us as churches succumb to the deceptive influence of the world. These are "Christians" whose ears have been closed to the truth of God's Word; buying into the lie that Bible interpretation and understanding is subject to change as social standards change. That is a new world order promoted by the spirit of antichrist, where there is no absolute truth.

We cannot know how to pray or intercede for the church if we are not willing to look squarely at what is happening; weakening and eroding faith in Christ and Him alone. Christ Jesus directs our attention to what He sees in His Revelation to the churches. If we ignore His admonition or dismiss it as not applying to "me or us", we become part of the problem. I use the pronoun "we" because we are the body of Christ, called to represent Him and His love for a world in darkness.

> *"There is one body and one Spirit, just as you were called in one hope of your calling: One Lord, one faith, one baptism; one God and Father of all, who is above all, and through all, and in you all"* (Ephesians 4:4-6).

The things that impact the body of Christ, should concern us.

The organized church has in many instances given in to social pressure both from within and without. The spirit of antichrist working overtime to exert influence in our churches, has been successful in diverting attention from the work of the cross and Holy Spirit to the causes of humanity and social acceptance. Embracing the all-inclusive message of the world is in direct opposition to the truth of God's Word.

When churches begin to subvert the Word of God to accommodate social reform, they are in trouble. When the message from the pulpit is stripped of its power to convince or convict the hearer of sin, the people are in trouble. If we are functioning as the Spirit filled body of Christ, we should find ourselves compelled to pray and intercede for a mighty move of His Spirit across the globe — while there is time. Oh that churches that name the name of Christ would shed the shackles of prosperity and success as defined by the world, the leg irons of social reform and once more embrace the message of the cross, of salvation and deliverance, Christ's victory over sin and death.

We know that everything happening in our world right now serves God's purpose: It is by way of preparation for Christ's return to set up His kingdom here on earth - His millennial reign from Jerusalem. May I encourage you as a believer "in Christ", to *"set your mind on things above"*, align your thoughts and will with that of Christ and pray *"...Your kingdom come, Your will be done..."* Pray for **the Church,** intercede for believers in every nation, that they be strengthened in the inner man, to be able to stand in the days ahead, steadfast and true. That is Christianity in action. To God be glory!

If per chance you are reading this book and you do not know Christ Jesus as your Savior and Lord, it is a simple matter of agreeing with God - that we are sinners apart from Him because of our sin nature, despite any natural goodness.

My prayer is that the Spirit of God would prepare your heart to accept by faith His provision in Christ for you, to restore you to fellowship with Him: Finding peace with God, forgiveness of sin and the assurance of eternal life. That together, we would have ears to hear - *"alle, alle, auch sind frei",* all, all, come in — in other words **"come home."**

Biography

Born in December 1937, in Lyons, New York, I was the third and last child. My mother's health was fragile, and she was warned against having more children after the first: But God had other plans.

Graduating from High School in 1956, followed by a four year stretch in the U.S. Navy, I thought my future was to leave my mark on the world as an artist: But God had other plans. I spent thirty-seven years working for international airlines as a Personnel, Human Resource Administrator - dealing with people and people problems: Enjoyed every minute of it.

With retirement, I left the New York City, metropolitan area and moved back to the homestead on Lake Ontario, looking forward to peace and quiet and time to focus on my art: But God had other plans. I pastored a church for ten years, seeing first-hand the need for biblical teaching and fellowship in the Word of God.

Having enjoyed writing all my life, prose, poetry and songs, I said I would never write a book. However, given the time in which we live and impressed by the Spirit of the Lord to write, this is offered as a labor of love. First and foremost, for Christ and His body, but also for those who are searching for answers, for security and peace in a world gone mad.

Forever thankful that God knows those that are His and spares nothing to have them for Himself.

Made in the USA
Middletown, DE
06 November 2021